Welcome

to the complete guide to the iPad 2…

Life without the iPad already seems a clunky distant past. Apple's brand new iPad 2 has only just arrived in the UK , and we've been working hard to deliver all the essential information you need to get the most out of the iPad phenomenon.

With the competition struggling to catch up with Apple's first iPad, Steve Jobs, Apple's CEO has changed the game with the iPad 2. Smaller, lighter and faster than its predecessor, and now in a choice of two colours: black or white, we think it's the best product Apple has ever made.

In this guide we will tell you all about what's under the hood, what's new, and how to use all the great new features found in the iPad 2.

This book explains how to get up and running without any hassle, how to explore new functions like FaceTime and Photo Booth, and all the secrets and tips you need to become an iPad 2 expert.

On top of that we'll introduce you to the greatest apps and accessories, so you really get the most out of owning an iPad 2.

So get ready for the next evolution to your iPad lifestyle – say hello to the iPad 2.

Mustafa Mustafa, Publishing Director

CONTACTS

Editor in chief	Mark Hattersley
020 7756 2879	mark_hattersley@idg.co.uk
Art director	Mandie Johnson
020 7756 2881	mandie_johnson@idg.co.uk
Sub editor	Lisa Giles-Keddie

ADDITIONAL CONTRIBUTORS
Christopher Breen, Rob Buckley, Fred Dutton, Jonny Evans, James Galbraith, Karen Haslam, Karl Hodge, Patrick Llewelyn-Davies, Alice Ross

PRODUCTION

Head of production	Richard Bailey
020 7756 2839	richard_bailey@idg.co.uk

CIRCULATION & MARKETING

Acting marketing manager	Emma van Beurden
	emma_vanbeurden@idg.co.uk

PUBLISHING

Publishing director	Mustafa Mustafa
	mustafa@idg.co.uk
Managing director	Kit Gould

The Complete Guide to iPad is a publication of IDG Communications, the world's leading IT media, research and exposition company. With more than 300 publications in 85 countries, read by more than 100 million people each month, IDG is the world's leading publisher of computer magazines and newspapers. IDG Communications, 101 Euston Road, London NW1 2RA. This is an independent journal not affiliated with Apple Computer. Apple, the Apple logo, Mac, and Macintosh are registered trademarks of Apple Computer. All contents © IDG 2010, except when © Mac Publishing LLC. Project management & print by Fusion Media – Tel: 03309 991 240, email: info@fusionmedialtd.co.uk

Official Angry Birds 3 Star Walkthrough Theme 1
' evels 16-21

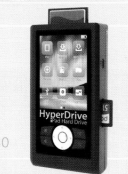

The complete guide…

6 Everything iPad
We explain why the iPad is the must-have gadget of the year, and outline its key features

Features

16 Your new digital lifestyle
How the iPad fills the gap between your phone and PC

20 iPad mythology
Was the iPad really in development for 18 years?

22 Exploring Settings
Get to grips with Settings – the iPad's real workhorse app

28 Speed-testing the iPad 2
Ready, steady, go! We test the iPad 2 against the original

Buyers guide

30 Hot iPad accessories
From cases to stands to styluses – check out the best add-ons

36 The 30 must-have apps
Add yet more functionality to your iPad with the finest apps

Final word

162 The iPad challenge
We look at what Apple should do next with the iPad 3.0

Tutorials

44 Plug and play

48 Browsing the internet

52 Using Photo Booth

56 FaceTime

60 Using Mail

64 Watching video

68 Using the iPod app

72 GarageBand

76 The iTunes Store

80 The App Store

84 iMovie

88 Calendar guided tour

92 Scheduling events

96 Using Contacts

100 Watching YouTube

104 Importing photos

Essential app tutorials

110 Pages

118 Numbers

126 Keynote

134 Bento

138 LogMeIn Ignition

142 Instapper

146 Brushes

150 TweetDeck

154 Things

158 Comics

Everything iPad 2

Your complete guide to the second coming of Apple's game-changing portable computing phenomenon

By Fred Dutton

What a year it's been for Apple. Rewind to January 2010, and naysayers were lining up to pour scorn on the just-unveiled iPad. "What's it for?" They asked. "It's just a giant iPhone," they insisted. Well, how very wrong they were. From that standing start, Apple's bold new creation has gone on to become a bona fide phenomenon, single-handedly redefining the tablet concept and carving out a huge market where many had argued one didn't really exist. It's the very definition of a must-have device, transforming the way we work, communicate and, of course, entertain ourselves.

And now, after months of speculation, its second iteration is finally upon us. Slimmer, sleeker and more powerful, the iPad 2 is all set to take the tablet to the next level. Over the next ten pages, we'll be talking you through the myriad refinements, improvements and smart new additions Apple has made to its game-changing gizmo. From its sleek new look and lightning fast CPU, to its twin cameras and exciting new apps, this is the only guide to the iPad 2 you'll ever need to read.

Redesigning a phenomenon

How the iPad conquered the world, and why Apple has gone back to the drawing board

A little over a year ago, the embryonic tablet market was limping. Early PC-based devices had failed to strike a chord with consumers. Critics complained they were pricey, unreliable and impractical.

Then, in January last year, Apple boss Steve Jobs took the wraps off the iPad. Those same pundits were sceptical, but the device immediately captured the public's imagination. Unlike much of the competition, it was very affordable, with prices starting from £329. Not only that but its slick, intuitive operating system was both immediately familiar to millions of Apple users and easily accessible to newcomers. With the App Store, it offered tens of thousands of applications for download.

The iPad was a phenomenon from day one and has since sold over 15 million units, rewarding Apple with a 90 per cent share of the entire tablet market. Developers have released 65,000 dedicated iPad apps – that's an average of around 180 new programs a day.

On top of all that, Apple's all-conquering gizmo has been adopted in schools as a learning aid, and by doctors, businessmen and creatives.

"It's amazing to think that just a year ago very few people had actually held an iPad in their hands," says Apple marketing chief Michael Tchao. "It truly has become a blockbuster post-PC device."

So, all eyes on its successor, the iPad 2. While its success is virtually assured, Apple's designers have fought complacency to introduce a number of important, intuitive new features that enhance the experience.

"2011 is clearly going to be the year of the iPad2"

"With iPad 2 we've made advances in form and function that are so significant and far-reaching," insists Jony Ive, Apple's senior design VP.

So what exactly are these changes? The iPad 2 is now slimmer, smaller and sleeker. It's 33 per cent thinner and 15 per cent lighter than its predecessor. According to Ive, "It's not only more comfortable to hold ... It's also rigid, sturdy and even more precise."

However, the iPad 2 is not only smaller, but also considerably more powerful. Its new dual core A5 processor is twice as fast as Apple's original tablet, offering up to nine times the graphics performance. This etxra oomph offers new experiences that were impossible on the first iPad. FaceTime brings videochat, GarageBand is a brilliant, fully-featured music creation studio, and Photo Booth is a fun, frothy picture editing app.

Pictures, you say? The iPad2 boasts two cameras, one facing back at you and the other facing forward. Both are capable of shooting video (the latter in HD) that you can edit in a new iOS version of Mac staple iMovie.

You can also now plug your iPad into an HD TV for real-time mirroring – perfect if you're presenting to the board, or want to share images or watch video content on the big screen. There's a gyroscope for further added functionality, too. The iPad now comes in white as well as black, while the new Smart Cover, detailed on page 10, is offered in ten different colours.

It's not quite a total revolution, but it's an impressive evolution that takes a game-changing gadget and makes it even more indispensable. As Apple CEO Steve Jobs put it while unveiling the new device in San Francisco last month, "2011 is clearly going to be the year of the iPad 2."

Get to know your way around the iPad 2

What the iPad 2 looks like and what it does

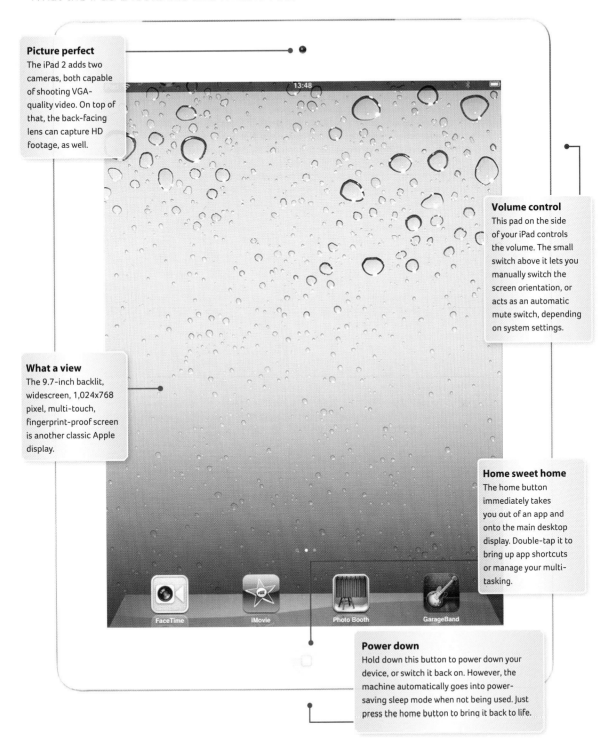

Picture perfect

The iPad 2 adds two cameras, both capable of shooting VGA-quality video. On top of that, the back-facing lens can capture HD footage, as well.

Volume control

This pad on the side of your iPad controls the volume. The small switch above it lets you manually switch the screen orientation, or acts as an automatic mute switch, depending on system settings.

What a view

The 9.7-inch backlit, widescreen, 1,024x768 pixel, multi-touch, fingerprint-proof screen is another classic Apple display.

Home sweet home

The home button immediately takes you out of an app and onto the main desktop display. Double-tap it to bring up app shortcuts or manage your multi-tasking.

Power down

Hold down this button to power down your device, or switch it back on. However, the machine automatically goes into power-saving sleep mode when not being used. Just press the home button to bring it back to life.

The **smartest** cover

Everything you need to know about Apple's ingenious new Smart Cover

One other new Apple innovation launches alongside the iPad 2 – the Smart Cover. On the face of it, a case might not seem like an awful lot to get excited about. But look a little closer, and you'll see it's a quietly innovative piece of design that represents a real leap on from the original device's first party slip case.

Available in ten differ colours (five in polyurethane for £35 each, and five in aniline-dyed leather for £59 each), the Smart Cover magnetically attaches to the side of the device. It can be folded back on itself to offer a stand for typing or viewing content, and automatically activates sleep mode when closed, or wakes the iPad up when opened. What's more, its microfibre internal lining helps buff the screen clean when it's shut.

"We wanted to figure out a way to protect the display without compromising the iPad's size and weight," explains Apple's design VP Jony Ive. "So, rather than developing a separate case, we created a cover at the same time that we were actually designing the iPad. The two are made to work together."

Clean and tidy
When closed, the perfectly aligned cover helps keep the iPad's screen clean, thanks to its space-age microfibre lining

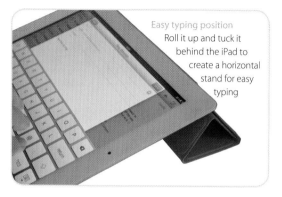

Easy typing position
Roll it up and tuck it behind the iPad to create a horizontal stand for easy typing

Hardback stand
You can snap the cover back on its magnetic hinge like a hardback book while using your iPad

Vertical viewing
...or a vertical stand perfect for watching video content or viewing picture slideshows

Switched on

Don't ask us how the magicians at Apple HQ came up with this one. When you open the cover, your iPad will immediately awaken from sleep mode without the need for tapping the home button. Then, when you close it again, your iPad will automatically hibernate again.

Ready-to-go device
The new Smart Cover does more than just protect your screen – it keeps your iPad ready-to-go

A magnetic attraction

The idea of a magnetic clip might seem a little flimsy at first but the Smart Cover resolutely holds fast, even when stuffed in an overnight bag or briefcase. It aligns perfectly with the outline of the device, thanks to magnets both in the spine of the iPad itself and in the frame of the cover.

Magnetic power
The Smart Cover sits perfectly aligned on your iPad, thanks to a sturdy set of magnets

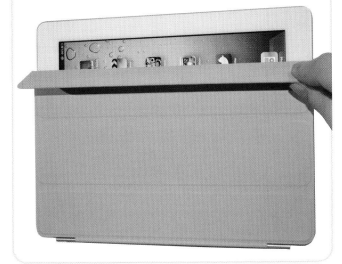

Looking good

Whereas the official Apple slipcase for the original iPad only came in a functional but rather spartan black, the design team has really gone to town on the iPad 2's cover. It's available in ten different colours. Five of these are available in sturdy polyurethane (costing £35), while another five come in classy aniline-dyed Italian leather (costing £59)

Splash of colour
Take your pick from ten vibrant colours and two different cover finishes

Accessories

Peripheral vision

Your guide to the official accessories that will help you get the most from your iPad 2

Apple keyboard

If you use your iPad as your primary portable computing device, you might want to invest in an Apple Keyboard Dock (£56). Although we prefer to use a regular Apple Bluetooth Keyboard, as shown (£57). It's smaller and lighter than the Keyboard Dock and transmits information wirelessly, you'll need a case to stand up the iPad though.

Keyboard options Apple's lightweight wireless bluetooth keyboard is compact enough to slip into your briefcase.

iPad 2 Dock

Though the Smart Cover offers a perfectly sturdy stand for your iPad, Apple's iPad 2 Dock (£26) adds a few more features. As well as a robust rest, it offers easy access to a port for charging or syncing. There's also an audio line-out port for connecting to speakers and it's compatible with the Camera Connection Kit, too.

Docking The iPad 2 Dock serves as a useful permanent charging station or audio streaming hub.

iPad Camera Connection Kit

Rather than forcing you to download digital photos from your camera onto a computer before transferring them across to your iPad, the Camera Connection Kit (£26) cuts out the middleman and lets you import pictures straight from your camera. An additional dongle also lets you download images straight from an SD card.

Camera Connection Kit Make importing photos onto your iPad even easier with the Camera Connection Kit.

Apple in-ear headphones with remote and mic

Does what it says on the tin. These in-ear headphones (£66) offer impressive sound isolation, two high performance drivers and a mid-cable remote that lets you control your iTunes library or video playback at the touch of a button. There's also a built-in mic on the remote for recording voice memos.

In-ear Perfect for silent running, these high-end in-ear headphones offer excellent clarity of sound.

Apple Digital AV Adaptor

The iPad 2 now allows you to mirror whatever is happening on-screen on your HD TV. To take advantage of the feature you'll need to pick up a Digital AV Adaptor. As well as letting you stream movies, music and other content to your TV, it also charges your iPad in the process.

Digital AV Adaptor View video, enjoy music or play games in HD.

Apps

The iPad 2 App Guide
The best iPad 2-only apps to put your gadget through its paces

FaceTime

Thanks to the iPad 2's new built-in camera, the iPhone 4's FaceTime application has been brought over to Apple's tablet. You can now videochat over wi-fi with any other iPad 2, iPhone 4, iPod touch or Mac. Just tap on their name in your contacts list and, provided they're online, an invitation will pop up on their screen.

FaceTime The iPad 2's new camera brings wi-fi video chat to the device for the first time.

GarageBand

Fancy yourself as a budding musician? Welcome to paradise. GarageBand (£2.99) is an addictive, feature-packed portable take on Apple's acclaimed Mac music-making software. It lets you record your own mini symphonies, either using your own instruments or the digital equivalents provided in-app.

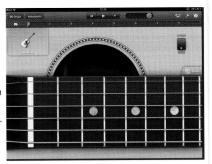

GarageBand It will take some time to get your head around it properly, but persevere and GarageBand offers a creative wonderland.

iMovie

Now you can shoot video with your iPad, courtesy of the exterior HD camera, it makes sense that Apple adds its film editing package to the App Store. Once you've shot your footage, you'll be able to edit it as a mini home movie masterpiece, then share it with friends.

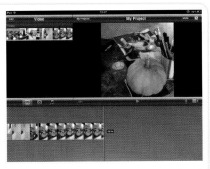

iMovie Like GarageBand, iMovie is a comprehensive distillation of its beefy desktop progenitor.

Photo Booth

It's not exactly Photoshop, but what Photo Booth lacks in features it makes up for in infectious fun. This free app simply lets you add weird and wonderful visual effects to your iPad snaps. Once you've captured a ridiculous self-portrait, you can then immediately share it with friends via email or Bluetooth.

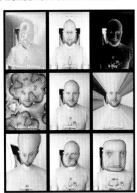

Photo Booth Photo Booth lets you add one of nine wacky special effects to your photos.

Infinity Blade

The iPad 2 offers new opportunities for game developers to push the envelope and deliver some truly gobsmacking experiences. Sword fighting epic Infinity Blade is one of the first games to step up to the plate, with a recent update adding optimised, crystal clear visuals exclusive to iPad 2 owners.

Infinity Blade iPad gaming gets a boost thanks to the powerful new A5 processor.

Under the hood – inside the **iPad 2**

The power behind the new evolution that boasts HD recording

185.7 mm

8.8 mm

241.2mm

Weight: 601g (613g for 3G model)

Twin cameras

The iPad 2 boasts two cameras, one on the back and one on the front. The front-facing lens can shoot VGA footage at up to 30 frames per second and take VGA quality stills. The rear facing camera captures 720p HD footage and boasts a 5x digital zoom. Apple hasn't released megapixel specs but don't expect anything too crisp – the cameras are functional rather than high end.

Capture the moment The iPad's two cameras might not offer top-of-the-line specs but add important functionality to the device

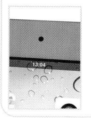

The Dual A5 Processor

While the original iPad was no slouch, its successor has been given a real dose of rocket fuel courtesy of Apple's new 1GHz dual A5 processor. That essentially means where once the iPad was powered by a single core chip, it now has two. Apps load faster, multi-tasking is that little bit smoother and browsing the web is lightning quick.

Faster, sharper apps
Your apps will look sharper and work faster thanks to the new dual A5 processor

Memory matters

Whereas the original iPad offered 256MB of system memory, Apple's new device has doubled that to 512MB. What this means for you? You can now run more apps at the same time and switch between them quicker. Not only that, but high-spec apps like GarageBand or Infinity Blade now run more smoothly too.

Memory doubled
Apple has doubled the amount of system memory in the iPad 2 to a sturdy 512MB, making it great for gaming and demanding apps like GarageBand

The **iPad 2** Specifications

Apple iPad 2

	iPAD 2 WIFI	iPAD 2 WIFI & 3G
Dimensions	241.2mm x 185.7 mm x 8.8 mm	241.2mm x 185.7 mm x 8.8 mm
Weight	601g	613g
Price	£399 (16GB); £479 (32GB); £599 (64GB)	£499 (16GB); £579 (32GB); £659 (64GB)
Wireless	Wi-fi; Bluetooth 2.1	Wi-Fi: UMTS/HSDPA/HSUPA (850, 900, 1,900, 2,100 MHz); GSM/EDGE (850, 900, 1,800, 1,900 MHz). Bluetooth 2.1
Display	9.7-inch LED-backlit glossy widescreen; multi-touch display with IPS technology; 1,024x768 pixel resolution at 132 pixels per inch	9.7-inch LED-backlit glossy widescreen; multi-touch display with IPS technology; 1,024x768 pixel resolution at 132 pixels per inch
Chip	1GHz dual-core Apple A5 processor	1GHz dual-core Apple A5 processor
Cameras	Back camera: 720p HD Video recording at 30 frames per second with audio; still camera with 5x digital zoom. Front camera: VGA video recording at 30 frames per second with audio; VGA-quality still camera	Back camera: 720p HD Video recording at 30 frames per second with audio; still camera with 5x digital zoom. Front camera: VGA video recording at 30 frames per second with audio; VGA-quality still camera
Battery	25-watt-hour rechargeable lithium-polymer battery offering around 10 hours of life	25-watt-hour rechargeable lithium-polymer battery offering around 10 hours of life
Input/output	30-pin dock connector port; 3.5-mm stereo headphone minijack; built-in speaker; microphone	30-pin dock connector port; 3.5-mm stereo headphone minijack; built-in speaker; microphone; micro-SIM card tray
Sensors	Three-axis gyro; accelerometer; ambient light sensor	Three-axis gyro; accelerometer; ambient light sensor
Location	Wi-fi triangulation; digital compass	Wi-fi triangulation; cellular network triangulation; assisted GPS; digital compass
Audio playback	Formats: HE-AAC (V1 and V2), AAC (8 to 320 Kbps), protected AAC (from iTunes Store), MP3 (8 to 320 Kbps), MP3 VBR, Audible (formats 2, 3, and 4, Audible Enhanced Audio, AAX, and AAX+), Apple Lossless, AIFF, and WAV. Dolby Digital 5.1 surround sound pass-through with Digital AV Adapter (sold separately)	Formats: HE-AAC (V1 and V2), AAC (8 to 320 Kbps), protected AAC (from iTunes Store), MP3 (8 to 320 Kbps), MP3 VBR, Audible (formats 2, 3, and 4, Audible Enhanced Audio, AAX, and AAX+), Apple Lossless, AIFF, and WAV. Dolby Digital 5.1 surround sound pass-through with Digital AV Adapter (sold separately)
Video playback	Formats: H.264 video up to 720p, 30 frames per second, Main Profile level 3.1 with AAC-LC audio up to 160 Kbps, 48kHz, stereo audio in .m4v, .mp4, and .mov file formats; MPEG-4 video, up to 2.5 Mbps, 640 by 480 pixels, 30 frames per second, Simple Profile with AAC-LC audio up to 160 Kbps per channel, 48kHz, stereo audio in .m4v, .mp4, and .mov file formats; Motion JPEG (M-JPEG) up to 35 Mbps, 1,280 by 720 pixels, 30 frames per second, audio in ulaw	Formats: H.264 video up to 720p, 30 frames per second, Main Profile level 3.1 with AAC-LC audio up to 160 Kbps, 48kHz, stereo audio in .m4v, .mp4, and .mov file formats; MPEG-4 video, up to 2.5 Mbps, 640 by 480 pixels, 30 frames per second, Simple Profile with AAC-LC audio up to 160 Kbps per channel, 48kHz, stereo audio in .m4v, .mp4, and .mov file formats; Motion JPEG (M-JPEG) up to 35 Mbps, 1,280 by 720 pixels, 30 frames per second, audio in ulaw
Comes with	Dock connector to USB cable, 10W USB power adapter, Documentation	Dock connector to USB cable, 10W USB power adapter, Documentation
Environmental requirements	Operating temperature: 0° to 35°C. Maximum operating altitude: 3,000m	Operating temperature: 0° to 35°C. Maximum operating altitude: 3,000m

Apple's new
digital lifestyle

The iPad is designed to plug the gap between the Mac and the iPhone – but is this marketing spin or genuine innovation?
By Christopher Breen

When Steve Jobs unveiled the iPad, he pronounced that it was a device designed to fit between the iPhone and the Mac in terms of functionality. Given the iPad's price and size, it would be easy enough to dismiss this as marketing hype. However, it's worth investigating the idea – because the notion of having a device with capabilities between those of your phone and your computer runs far deeper than a Keynote presentation and press release.

In fact, when using the iPad, you find a hybridisation of the iPhone and Mac operating sytems just about everywhere you turn. Certainly elbow-room plays a part – the device offers the kind of space that allows more elements on screen – but it's interesting to wade into the device and its applications and see where Apple expanded as well as compromised between the iPhone and Mac.

The personal organization applications – Mail, Contacts, and Calendar – owe more to the Mac OS than the iPhone. This is largely because of the roominess of the iPad's display. But there are other areas where the mobility of the iPhone makes it more of your go-to device. Apps such as National Rail and traffic information apps are best used out of the pocket, rather than out of your bag and cradled in your elbow joint.

It's a date Some apps, such as Calendar, benefit hugely from the iPad's large screen

Getting into the software

The personal organiser tools on the iPad are a real strength of the device. In Mail, the iPad's large screen means that you can view a list of mailboxes within a particular account or a list of messages along with a preview of a selected message, much like Mail on the Mac. Unlike with the Mac's version of Mail, you're still compelled to move to a separate screen to view all your accounts (a unified Inbox is absent, though it should be available with a software update later this year).

Stay in contact Contacts appear within a book-like interface that falls somewhere between the iPhone's Contacts app and OS X's Address Book. As with the iPhone app, you can move through an alphabetical list of contacts by tapping letters – though in this case, they're tabs in an address book rather than letters floating on-screen with no context. Like the Mac's Address Book, you can view contact names along with the details of the selected contact on a single screen. The compromise in this app is that you choose Groups by tapping a 'Groups' button, which produces a pop-up menu for selecting the group you want to view. On the Mac, groups aren't hidden in a pop-up menu.

> The notion of a device to sit between your Mac and your iPhone runs deeper than marketing hype

Track your diary The Calendar app is very similar to desktop-based iCal. In Day view you see not only events laid out in iCal-like blocks, but also the details of specific appointments, which appear on the left side of the 'book'. Week view looks very much like iCal, complete with a pop-up Details window. And from within any of these views you can tap on a calendar's button and choose which calendars to view.

Just browsing Safari, too, owes more to the Mac OS than the iPhone. When visiting a website that offers both mobile and desktop versions of the site, you see the desktop version. Yet the iPhone's double-tap-to-expand-columns trick works on the iPad. The display is large enough that you can have navigation and bookmark controls next to the URL fields rather than at the bottom of the screen. To view bookmarks, you can simply tap a 'Bookmarks' icon to reveal a Bookmarks menu pop-up, much like a pull-down menu in the Mac OS. And the iPad version of Safari even includes a bookmarks bar-like feature that provides quick access to favorite sites.

Find your way There's nothing like Maps outside of a browser on the Mac OS, so naturally the iPad's version of this helpful application is quite

Just browsing Using your fingers to browse the internet is more intuitive than using a mouse

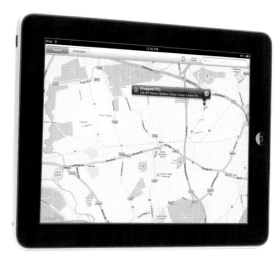

similar to the iPhone's version. But again, screen space pays off. Directions are available from a pop-up menu that appears over the map view you've selected (this version of Maps includes a new Terrain view). Like the iPhone 3GS, the iPad's Maps app includes compass capabilities, even though the iPad doesn't offer a separate Compass app. The size of the device limits its practicality in this area though – it'll be easier to navigate with an iPad in a car than on foot.

Sense of direction
Maps on the iPad looks great, but is more unwieldy than on the iPhone

iPad as iPod

The iPod and Videos apps are an interesting mix of the iPhone and Mac OS. In terms of browsing your media, they're very much like the Mac and PC version of iTunes. Similar to iTunes on a computer, you find your audio content available in a Source list, which includes Music, Podcasts, Audiobooks, iTunes U, Genius, Genius Mixes, and then any playlists you've synced from your computer or created on the iPad. Buttons at the bottom of the screen let you view your music by Song, Artist, Album, Genre or Composer. To play a track, just tap it.

Video content As with iTunes, videos are selected by kind – Movies, TV Shows, Podcasts, Music Videos, and iTunes U. Tap the 'TV Shows' button, for example, and you see each show represented by its artwork.

When you select a movie, you first see a screen filled with details – rating, studio, year released, HD or SD, summary, actors, director, and producers. On this same screen you can tap a Chapters button to see a list of chapters. To play a particular chapter, tap it and press the Play button.

Yet when you play music or watch videos, it's a very iPhone-like experience. Play a song, for example, and the iPad's screen is filled with album artwork along with volume and play controls, a button for producing a tracklist, and a Genius button for creating a Genius Playlist based on the currently playing song. Tap the artwork and you see a timeline (which you can scrub through just as you can with an iPhone or iPod touch) and shuffle and repeat buttons.

Playing video is an experience identical to that on an iPhone or iPod touch. Play controls are overlaid on the display when you tap it and the top of the display bears a timeline (which, again, you can scrub through) and a button for toggling between fullscreen and widescreen views.

Smarter shopping The iTunes Store is cramped on an iPhone or iPod touch. On the iPad, it's very much like the Store you see when using a Mac or PC. You can more easily find the content you're after than you can on the iPhone thanks to the Music, Movies, TV Shows, Podcasts, Audiobooks, and iTunes U buttons at the bottom of the screen. And you can see more information about the media you're interested in.

Credit where it's due
Lock up your credit card – buying media on the iPad is easy as pie

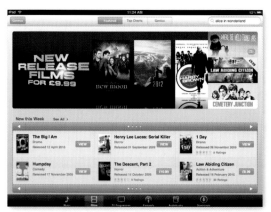

The missing apps

When viewing the iPad's home screen you can't help
but notice just how spare it appears. And it is, in part, because
it's missing a number of apps found on the iPhone and iPod
touch – Stocks, Weather, Voice Memos, Clock, and Calculator.
Many people have offered theories as to why these apps
didn't make the cut. One is that third-party apps exist for
these things, so why would Apple need to
duplicate these efforts? That makes
some sense. But it also makes
sense that in a world where you
can carry both an iPhone and iPad, the
iPhone does a better job presenting these small-form
applications. How weather-obsessed must you be to want to see radar,
satellite, precipitation, and forecast data on a single screen? These are
apps that you want to check for quick updates, not in-depth information.

Hot desking The
laptop has its
advantages for iTunes,
but the mobile iTunes
interface is easy to use

Oversized There's no
calculator on the iPad
– you use your iPhone
for that

Neither big iPod touch nor MacBook

Once you've used an iPad you understand just how silly the
'it's nothing but a big iPod touch' claim is. Size matters. It's much more
enjoyable to watch video on an iPad. You can read on the thing in a way
that doesn't feel cramped. The increased size means fewer finger swipes
and taps because you can put more controls and information on a single
screen. And it's less likely you're going to get
killed in some shoot-'em-up because you
tapped the wrong pixel of the device's display.

No laptop At the same time, the iPad in
its current form isn't a laptop replacement.
In portrait orientation you still have to two-
finger type. Landscape orientation, is better,
but there's the problem of punctuation. You
won't find apostrophes and quotation marks
on the main keyboard. Instead you have to
tap the '.?123' key to access this punctuation.

Beyond typing, there are things the iPad just
won't do that many laptop users find necessary.
Obviously, with its limited storage, memory, and
input options, you're not going to do Final Cut
work on your iPad any time soon. Nor is this the device to use for recording
your next podcast. But there are more mundane chores that the iPad can't
handle – printing, for example. Apple
provides no solution. The iPad as the
sole computing device in the home is
still a stretch.

Know your audience But the
idea of the iPad sitting between the
iPhone and the computer works
– it seems like a perfect fit. It's an
extravagant world in which we all
have a computer for computing, a
smartphone for phoning, and an
iPad for everything else, but if you
actually get to try this set-up it's hard
to fault it. It's more productive than
just an iPhone and a computer, and
it's more fun, too.

Type cast The onscreen
keyboard can't compete
with the real thing

TV times The iPad's
beautiful screen
is perfect for watching
YouTube videos

iPad
mythology

Investigating the decade of rumour and intrigue that led to the iPad's invention

By Mark Hattersley

iPad

The myth of an Apple Tablet is so firmly entrenched in the company's folklore that long before Apple announced the iPad there were entire websites devoted to it. For ten years now people have been discussing this product like it's the Third Coming. By January 2010, just about everybody in the tech industry was convinced that Apple had taken the iPod touch and created a great big 10in version, and for once Apple wasn't about to be contrary.

But the history of the rumour is interesting, because it suggests two possibilities. Either Apple has been working behind closed doors on the iPad for a decade, or the company has responded to the fervour for the device by actually creating it.

In May 2001, Kevin Fox, a lead designer at Google, said on his blog: "at least five times in the past ten years engineers at Apple have worked on initiatives to bring a full-sized tablet-based computer to market. Though the previous four attempts never saw the light of day, Apple has saved the best for last. This July: Meet iPad". That was ten years ago, and the myth has been circulating ever since.

The tablet rumours really returned en masse when netbook-style

A mysterious history – an iPad timeline

May 2001 Kevin Fox, a lead designer at Google, writes a blog entry called 'The Next Big Thing' that claims Apple is bringing a tablet PC called the iPad to market in July.

Nov 2001 Bill Gates demos a Microsoft Tablet PC at COMDEX. Rumour has it that Apple will follow.

Sep 2002 Steve Jobs tells *International Herald Tribune*: "We're not sure the tablet PC will be successful. It's turned into a notebook you can write on. Do you want to handwrite all your email?"

August 2004 *The Register* re-ignites the tablet rumour by reporting on an Apple handheld computer trademark registered in Europe.

April 2005 *Tablet PC Review* reports that the iPad is due in June 2005, claiming Apple has demonstrated it to select journalists at the Apple Store in Las Vegas.

Jan 2006 A US patent reveals an Apple device based upon an accelerometer.

Dec 2008 Rumours of a large-format iPod touch device similar to a tablet surface on website *Tech Crunch*, citing three sources.

April 2009 Apple COO Tim Cook says: "People looking for a small device that has internet access might consider an iPod touch or iPhone."

Sep 2009 *Gizmodo* says Apple is in talks with the *New York Times* about content for a "new device navigated without keyboard or mouse".

Nov 2009 Apple patent for a handheld computer with both pen and touch-based input appears on the US Patent and Trademark Office website.

Nov 2009 Chinese newspaper *Digitimes* reports that Apple is waiting for OLED displays and that the tablet will launch in the second half of 2010.

Dec 2009 A tablet-friendly edition of *Sports Illustrated* is demonstrated. An Apple patent emerges that appears to outline a process for making and selling digital magazines, books and other media.

Jan 2010 Apple announces the iPad at its headquarters in California.

computers arrived on the scene. Steve Jobs dismissed netbooks saying, "we don't know how to make a sub $500 computer that isn't junk", but also tellingly said: "We'll wait and see how that nascent category evolves."

The netbook's rise was coupled with a rise in the popularity of ebook readers. Although these remain relatively niche, the market for ebooks was causing monumental shifts in the publishing industry – and following the success of the iTunes Store for music and movies, Apple was prime suspect when it came to bringing the electronic bookstore to the masses.

Apple has shied away from calling the iPad a 'tablet computer', possibly because tablet computers have been around for a while and are seen as very niche products. The iPad isn't meant as a niche product at all. Apple hoped to hit a huge market – and it didn't want the iPad associated with an established product category because Apple was pitching it as the first step towards the future of mainstream computing, not a glossy revision of the past.

Patent pending

Here are some of Apple's patent applications that kept Mac fans guessing right up until the iPad was announced. They may have been red herrings, but the iPad emerged eventually…

Tablet Keyboard – This patent demonstrates a large virtual keyboard in action.

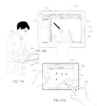

Using the tablet This clearly shows a large hand-held device in use with a multi-touch interface.

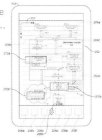

Tablet system This patent outlines touchscreen input and handwriting recognition.

Settings:
under the iPad's hood

The iPad works thrillingly as soon as you take it out of the box, but if you want to get the best out of it and customise it fully, you'll need to become an expert in the Settings app. Here's how…

By Dan Moren

Perhaps you're only interested in the jaw-dropping apps on your iPad – whiz-bang games and apps such as Mail and Safari that work just like on a desktop computer. But if you want to know what the iPad is really capable of, you'll have to dig deep into its real workhorse app: Settings.

Settings is where the magic happens, where you can do things beyond the capability of even the most powerful third-party iPad app. If you want to put your personal stamp on your iPad and delve into its cleverest capabilities, then Settings is your friend. Of course, if you're familiar with the iPhone or iPod touch, you'll find the iPad experience similar – it's running a very similar operating system after all. We took a stroll through the Settings app on the iPad to see how it differs and what's new.

Split personality

First, the interface. Settings uses the split-pane view that's become so familiar to iPad users, from Mail and Notes. In Settings' left pane, you'll find a list of the different categories of system settings and settings for apps (both built-in and third-party). On the right are the contents of whatever section you're currently viewing.

As with Mail, this change represents a big improvement over the corresponding iPhone app. To access some of the iPhone's settings, you have to drill down many levels and then head all the way back up again. On the iPad, having the top level of navigation always available is great for jumping back and forth.

Having the top level of navigation always available is great for jumping back and forth

Apple has clearly taken the time to ensure most sections don't require you to dive more than one level down: for more involved tasks (setting up mail accounts, for example, or most tasks that require you to enter text), a dialog box will often pop up in the middle of the screen. This approach has the benefit of making sure that you don't get lost in the interface: the rest of Settings is still clearly visible, though dimmed, behind the dialog window.

Organizationally, there have been some changes, too: the iPhone's Brightness and Wallpaper sections have been combined into one; Sounds now lives under General; and settings for third-party apps are now more clearly delineated. Otherwise, though, it looks pretty similar to the iPhone's Settings in most places.

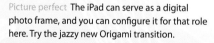

Picture perfect The iPad can serve as a digital photo frame, and you can configure it for that role here. Try the jazzy new Origami transition.

Push off Do you find you're getting lots of annoying notifications from apps and you don't know why? Toggle them on and off here.

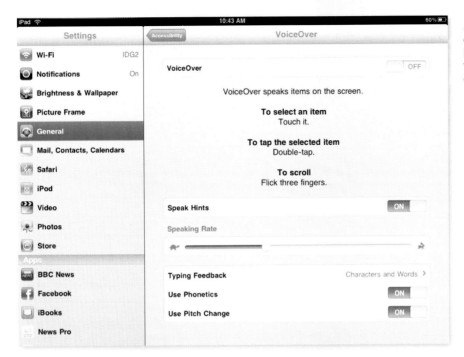

Accessibility To turn on VoiceOver and invert the screen to White on Black, go to General →Accessibility.

What's new

The iPad's not the iPhone, so there are plenty of new options as well as a few missing features. And there are obviously some differences between the WiFi-only and the 3G iPad models.

A brand new top-level section, Picture Frame, lets you set up the iPad's digital photo frame feature, which you can access from the device's lock screen. You can choose between two transitions – the classic Dissolve and a nifty folding Origami effect – and select whether you want the slideshow to use all of your photos, or just certain albums or events.

You also have the option to shuffle your photos, and, if you've picked the Dissolve transition, you can choose to have the photos zoomed in on detected faces (which is occasionally amusing, given Apple's sometimes shaky face-detection technology). The Origami transition automatically frames shots on faces, which is a cool touch.

As mentioned above, Brightness & Wallpaper combines two sections from the iPhone's Settings app. But what's really new here is that you can choose a background not only for the iPad's lock screen, but also for your home screen.

Mail, Contacts, and Calendars are virtually identical on the iPhone and iPad, although the WiFi-only iPad obviously doesn't allow you to import contacts from a SIM card.

Safari's preferences now have a toggle switch to always show the browser's Bookmarks Bar. Strangely, the Plug-Ins slider from the iPhone has disappeared.

Under iPod settings, you won't find the iPhone's Shake to Shuffle feature, and the iPad has broken out the video preferences to a separate Video section, though it contains the same functions.

The transition choices that appear in the iPhone's Photos settings have moved to the iPad's much more capable Photos app.

General contains the iPad's system-wide settings. The WiFi-only model lacks the iPhone's Usage sub-menu, but it adds the Sounds subsection, which itself loses phone-related features such as Vibrate, Ringtone, New Text Message, New Voicemail, and so on.

Under the Network subsection, you'll find the iPad has the same VPN and WiFi menus as the iPhone, and of course the WiFi-only model doesn't have either the iPhone 3GS's Enable 3G or Data Roaming toggles. If you have set up a VPN connection, you'll be able to toggle it on or off from the top-level Settings list in the left-hand pane.

The Auto-Lock options have changed slightly, as befits the iPad's more capacious battery: instead of the iPhone's never and one to five minute options, the iPad starts at two minutes, with options for five, 10 or 15 minutes, in addition to never locking.

There aren't any surprises in the iPad's Settings app, though expect it to change when the OS updates

Under Passcode, you'll mainly find the same options as on the iPhone, minus the 3GS's Voice Dial option and with a new slider to turn the Picture Frame feature on or off.

The Home button options are slightly altered from the iPhone: you can't set double-clicking the Home button to Phone Favorites or Camera, naturally, but otherwise they're identical.

Under Date & Time, the WiFi-only iPad doesn't let you set the time automatically, though this might be possible in the 3G version.

The Keyboard options have been rearranged slightly: there's now a sub-option under International Keyboards to change the keyboard layout for both the software and hardware keyboards. With the English keyboard,

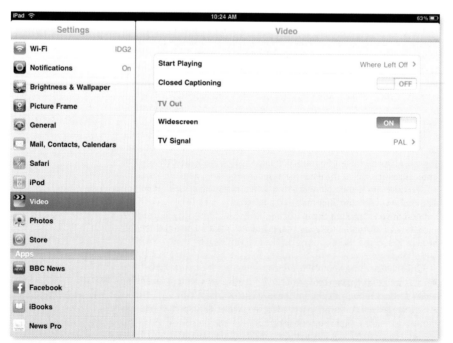

TV times To hook your iPad up to a UK television set to watch videos, you'll need to set the iPad to PAL output.

Hidden features Can't find a setting on an app you're using? It might have its settings hidden in the Settings app – check your Apps list here.

On Safari The Safari web browser is much richer than it first appears, and you have plenty of scope for customising your browsing in the Safari settings.

you can change the layout from the default QWERTY to AZERTY or QWERTZ, and you can have the hardware keyboard set up as US, Dvorak, US International – PC, US Extended, British, French, German, Spanish – ISO, Italian, Dutch, and Belgian.

The iPad's international keyboard options are far more limited than the iPhone's, with only 12 choices in addition to the US layout: Chinese (Simplified) Handwriting, Chinese (Simplified) Pinyin, Dutch, English (UK), Flemish, French, French (Canada), German, Italian, Japanese, Russian, and Spanish. However, when you add those additional keyboards, you often have the choice of several different hardware and software keyboard layouts. For example, under Russian you can set the hardware keyboard layout to Russian – PC, Russian, and Russian – Phonetic.

The iPad lacks the iPhone 3GS's Voice Control feature, so it's no surprise the Voice Control language options are missing under the International section. And if you want to change your iPad's whole interface to a different language, you'll find considerably fewer options than on the iPhone: the iPad only offers English, French, German, Japanese, Dutch, Italian, Spanish, Chinese and Russian. Expect these choices to increase as the iPad is released in more and more markets.

Accessibility is pretty similar to the 3GS, though the VoiceOver section adds options for using phonetics and pitch change.

And the iPad also has the same toggle to show the battery percentage monitor as the iPhone 3GS does; you'll find it under the General section.

Set it and forget it
There aren't any particularly earth-shaking surprises in the iPad's Settings app, though expect it to change as the operating system gets updated and Apple brings new features to the iPad. For now, the addition of the split-pane interface makes Settings much easier to navigate, especially when it comes to making quick changes on the move.

Power up The faster processor has a huge impact on power intensive apps like GarageBand

Speed testing the iPad 2

Faster, sleeker and more fun than before… we speed test the iPad 2
Jason Snell

The iPad 2 looks amazingly responsive in Apple's product demos, and the company's claims for its battery life are also impressive. But how does it perform in the real world? We've had a go on the iPad in our labs and we're happy to report that the battery actually performed well beyond Apple's claims..

The iPad 2 uses a new Apple-designed processor called the A5, which is making its first appearance on the scene. Apple is generally cagey about tech specs for products like the iPhone and iPad, but by all accounts, the A5 is a dual-core version of the 1GHz A4 chip that powers the iPhone 4 and the original iPad. The iPad 2 also has 512MB of RAM—twice that of the original iPad—and a 200MHz bus speed, likewise twice that of the original.

Because the A5 is a dual-core processor, Apple claims the iPad 2 can run at speeds up to double that of the original iPad. As with any dual-core processor, the key about "up to double" is that software must be optimized to take advantage of multiple processor cores, or that speed goes to waste. This is the first dual-core processor to appear on an iOS device, and it'll be interesting to see under what circumstances the A5 is noticeably faster than the A4, and when it's not.

But processor speed isn't the only part of the system that determines how it performs. Graphics performance has become a major component in determining how fast a computing device feels. And Apple says that the graphics performance on the iPad 2 is as much as nine times faster than on the original iPad.

So does the iPad 2 measure up to Apple's claims? Absolutely, though it's hard to determine whether the dual-core processor or the improved graphics performance deserve the credit. (Maybe the question is moot.) From the moment I started using the iPad 2 with familiar apps from my original iPad, I could tell that the system was faster. I thought scrolling through tweets in Twitterrific on my iPad was smooth as can be ... until I scrolled through the tweet list on the iPad 2. Everything felt smoother, and items loaded faster.

Get real Games like Real Racing 2 HD take full power of the iPad 2's improved functionality

Credit where it's due

Part of the speed boost, especially when I started to test performance in Safari, probably needs to be credited to iOS 4.3, which ships with the iPad 2 and includes a dramatic improvement to Safari's JavaScript engine. When I installed the golden master version of iOS 4.3 on an original iPad, performance improved as well. But even when both devices were running iOS 4.3, the iPad 2 was 1.6 times as fast as the original in running the SunSpider JavaScript test, and 1.9 times as fast as an iPhone 4 running the iOS 4.3 golden master.

In short, the iPad 2 is the fastest iOS device ever made, by a long shot. And it's not just an academic distinction: you can sense the speed when you use it, because everything's faster and smoother than it was on the original iPad.

Despite the boosts in processing power, Apple claims that the iPad 2 has the same ten-hour battery life as the original model. In nearly a week of use, I never saw a reason to disbelieve the claims. The iPad's all-day battery life, perhaps its killer feature, remains intact.

iPad and iPhone speed, graphics & battery life tests

	Sunspider	Startup	Framerate	nytimes.com	GarageBand Launch	GarageBand Import	GarageBand Send to Email	Battery life (minutes)
iPad 2 3G	**2.1**	**26**	**45**	**8**	**5**	**27**	**22**	**504**
iPad 1 3G	3.3	34	6.4	16	7	52	25	490
iPad 1 WiFi (iOS 4.2.1)	8.1	25	6.4	14	N/A	N/A	N/A	N/A
iPhone 4	4.0	46	7.2	16	N/A	N/A	N/A	272
iPhone 4 (iOS 4.2.)	10.1	36	N/A	16	N/A	N/A	N/A	N/A

Best results are in bold. Results are in seconds and lowest result is best. Apart from framerate which uses the GLBenchmark 2.0.3 app on the Egypt setting to measure how many frames per second are displayed (higher is better), and battery life, which is measured in minutes and highest result is best. All devices were tested using iOS 4.3 (apart from the iPhone 4 with iOS 4.2 for reference). Sunspider is a WebKit JavaScript performance test with results in seconds. Web Page test measured number of seconds to load www.nytimes.com in its entirety

20
Hot iPad

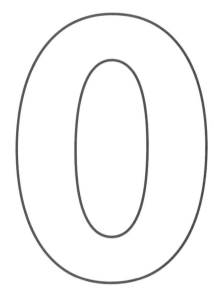

accessories

What could be better than an iPad? The answer: an iPad with all the right accessories. We pick the best extras and add-ons from the current crop

By Karl Hodge

Like all the best devices, the iPad is what you make it. For some people it'll be a photo viewer, for others a handy game system. Some folks will use it as an e-reader, while their mates might watch the latest movies on it. With its versatility, the iPad will soon become one of the most accessorised devices on the market.

From protective sleeves to speakers, via bespoke bags and stands, the number of accessories already announced is huge. That's before you even start to count the iPhone and iPod accessories that also work with the iPad – though we hasten to add that not all of them do.

So many types of accessory are possible, too. The iPad's conductive screen and large display makes it a great drawing tool, for example. All you need is a precision stylus. As for photos, the iPad doubles as a brilliant digital frame when not in active use. A stand will come in handy when you want to show off your family pics, and Apple's Camera Connection Kit will help you put them onto your iPad. Who knows what other kinds of accessory will emerge as new apps come out?

To give you a flavour of what's coming to market now, we've dug through the first wave of third-party extras, alongside the best that Apple has to offer, and highlighted our favourites. Many are already available, though a few are so new and fresh that they've yet to have an official release. Which will you pick to make your iPad the perfect purchase?

HyperMac HyperDrive Hard Drive For iPad

Company: HyperMac
URL: www.hyperdrive.com/ipad
Price: 320GB - £149 ; 500GB - £179; 1TB - £229

The HyperDrive is an ingenious hard drive that you can connect to your iPad, allowing you to carry your entire library of photos, music and video files, and to transfer your files onto the iPad, even when you're away from your computer. Available in sizes up to 1TB, the HyperDrive connects to the iPad via Apple's Camera Connection Kit. The contents of the HyperDrive appear on the iPad's screen, making it easy to transfer files accross.

Journey Bag for Apple iPad

Company: M-Edge
URL: www.medgestore.com
Price: $64.99 (£43)

Eager to project a more carefree image? These satchel-style bags might be more your thing. Made in nylon with a fluffy fleece interior to protect your iPad, they offer pockets for accessories as well as room for your charger. There's even a secret compartment lurking in the front flap.

Apple Digital AV Adaptor

Company: Apple
URL: www.apple.com
Price: £35

The iPad 2 enables you to play movies, show of photos, and display presentations on a big screen for the first time. To hook up an iPad 2 to a high definition TV, you'll need one of these. The second socket lets you charge up the iPad 2 at the same time.

Apple Smart Cover

Company: Apple
URL: www.apple.com
Price: £35

Many people will opt for this Apple Smart Cover, which clips magentically to the side of the iPad 2 and protects the screen from scratches. It's clever too, with microfibre inner that cleans the screen, and it switches the iPad 2 on and off as you open and close the flap. We're not convinced it'll save you from dents if accidentally drop the iPad 2 though.

Sena ZipBook for iPad

Company: Sena
URL: www.substrata.net
Price: £65

If the Smart Cover doesn't offer enough protection for you, then consider going all the way to this Sena ZipBook. It's made from leather and enables you to cover your iPad in a complete housing that will protect it against all drops, scratches, and scuffles.

HyperMac HyperDrive iPad Hard Drive

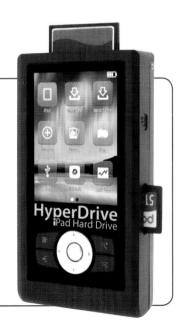

Company: HyperMac
URL: www.hyperdrive.com/ipad
Price: 320GB - £275; 500GB - £305; 750GB - £365

The second model in the HyperDrive range is even more ingenious than the first. Like the basic HyperDrive, this model connects to your iPad using Apple's Camera Connection Kit, allowing you to easily store and transfer all your music, photos and video files onto the iPad. However, this model also has two slots for reading memory cards, as well as a 3.2" LCD screen for browsing photos, which makes it a great back-up tool for photographers.

Apple iPad Keyboard Dock

Company: Apple
URL: www.apple.com/ipad
Price: £57

Anti-iPad whingers have focused on how difficult it is to type on the device. Well, there are a couple of options available to help you do  that, with Apple's own iPad Keyboard Dock expressly designed to make data input and writing easier. It looks great – and let's hope there are apps to do it justice.

BTKey

Company: Macally
URL: www.macally.com
Price: £59

Macally have launched a range of iPad accessories – but their BTKey keyboard isn't specifically for the iPad. Bluetooth-enabled, this is a full-sized QWERTY keyboard which couples with your iPad to add full typing capability. Unlike the Apple Keyboard Dock, it has a full numeric keypad, too.

Flex Stand for Apple iPad

Company: M-Edge
URL: www.medgestore.com
Price: $29.99 (£20)

Part iPad case, part tripod, this stand has flexible legs which enable you to orient your iPad in portrait or landscape mode. We're rather worried that, were we to own one, we'd want to throw it across the room to see if it's self-righting. Which it definitely isn't.

Cinema Seat

Company: Griffin
URL: www.griffintechnology.com
Price: $49.99 (£31)

Keep the kids entertained by using this nifty gadget to attach an iPad 2 to the rear of your car headrest. On the rear is a large strap that enables you to hook it to your car seat. This turns it into an instant in-car television system for the kids in the back. Pop on a movie and drive in peace as the iPad keeps them entertained.

HyperMac Stand

Company: HyperMac
URL: www.hypermac.com/stand
Price: £109.99

The iPad has great battery life, but it could still run flat if you're using it away from home or on a long plane flight. The HyperMac Stand is doubly useful as it's a handy pocket-sized stand that allows you to tilt the iPad at two different angles for reading or watching videos. It's also got a built-in battery pack that allows you to charge the iPad for up to 16 extra hours.

WaterGuard Waterproof Case for iPad

Company: Trendy Digital
URL: www.trendydigital.com
Price: £18.99

It looks a bit like a clear plastic bag for your iPad – and that's pretty much what this is. A low-tech solution for keeping your iPad splash-free in wet environments, the WaterGuard has a couple of press-studs which seal it shut. A shoulder strap is included.

iWrap

Company: Virtuosity Products
URL: www.getiwrap.com
Price: $29.95 (£20)

Worried about getting greasy smears on your iPad? iWrap is special plastic film, pre-cut to fit, that you stick to your iPad's screen and base. The process seems a bit fiddly, but once applied, the iWrap will protect your iPad from the elements.

Travel Vest

Company: Scottevest
URL: www.scottevest.com
Price: $100 (£65)

This isn't what we would call a vest – just as well, as the idea of a string undergarment with an iPad pocket is too strange even for us. We'd call this a body-warmer, one of whose 22 pockets is designed to fit an iPad. It's outdoorsy and geeky at the same time.

Hip Bag

Company: M-Edge
URL: www.medgestore.com
Price: $49.99 (£33.33)

Available in the same colours as M-Edge's range of sleeves, this messenger-style bag is blokey without being macho. Made from tough double-layered canvas treated with Scotchgard to make it water-repellent, it features leather detailing, too, making it a great choice for iPad-using hipsters.

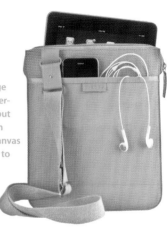

HyperMac Mini/Micro Battery Packs

Company: HyperMac
URL: www.hypermac.com
Price: Micro - £69.99; £89.99

HyperMac recently updated its iPad battery packs, giving them the same powerful battery as its MacBook rechargers. There are two versions available and a choice of ten eye-catching colours. The Micro battery pack measures just 1.6cm thick, and can power your iPad for an additional five hours, while the Mini is only slightly larger but doubles the battery life to an extra ten hours. They can charge an iPhone, too, as well as other devices such as digital cameras.

iSP150 Speaker Bar

Company: iLuv
URL: www.i-luv.com
Price: £21.50

The iPad's speakers haven't won that many fans in early reviews – so will this auxiliary speaker do the trick? Its makers claim the Speaker Bar produces clear sound and is fully mobile. It plugs into the iPad's headphone socket.

Bluetooth Music Receiver

Company: Belkin
URL: www.belkin.com
Price: £22

Need more welly than a dock or an external speaker can provide? Just connect this clever receiver to your home hi-fi and send music to it from your iPad by Bluetooth – you'll have as much wattage as your amp can provide. Tested with the iPad by Macworld in the US, it's designed for any Bluetooth-enabled media device.

PowerJolt for iPad

Company: Griffin
URL: www.griffintechnology.com
Price: £16.99

If you need to charge your iPad in the car, then Griffin's PowerJolt for iPad should do the trick. Unlike some other USB-based chargers, this gadget has plenty of juice, delivering 2.1 amps at 5 volts when plugged into your car's lighter socket. It ships with its own dock cable.

iPad Camera Connection Kit

Company: Apple
URL: www.apple.com/ipad
Price: £26

This has caused a bit of a stir among reviewers, as it features the only known adaptors between the iPad Dock connector and USB and SD devices. Use it to transfer content from digital cameras in any of the formats the iPad supports.

The
30 best apps

Our picks from the iPad App Store's gems…

By Mark Hattersley

The word 'app' was once just a nerdy abbreviation used by IT bods and sweaty gamers. Since the iPhone took the term as its own, though, it's become as ubiquitous as Tesco. The iPad launches a new phase of the app's bid for world domination. While iPhone apps are all about getting information quickly into the palm of your hand, the iPad allows the user an easier, more visual and less pressured experience. Already, the result of this shift is genuinely innovative games and apps. Here's our pick of the bunch so far.

Games

Infinity Blade

Price: £5.99

In Infinity Blade you must fight your way through the God King's lair and avenge your father's death. The game is a linear adventure where you fight numerous one-on-one battles with the God King's henchmen by swiping across the screen to attack and dodge your enemies. Visually stunning and perfect for the iPad's large touch display.

Rating: ★★★★★

Superbrothers: Sword and Sworcery

Price: £2.99

A wonderfu action adventure game with a truly superb retro visual style. In Sword and Sworcery adventure through levels solving musical puzzles to a score composed by Jim Guthrie, and the graphics were designed by Superbrothers. An enchanting experience and one of the best iPad games yet.

Rating: ★★★★★

Scrabble for iPad

Price: £5.99

The one-player mode is still infuriating and the artificial intelligence rubbish, but the multi-player mode suits the iPad's large screen perfectly. It even comes with a free iPhone app that players can use as virtual tile-holders, from which you can flick your letters to the board. An expensive way to replicate a board, but novel nonetheless.

Rating: ★★★★

Specifically designed to take advantage of the iPad 2, Real Racing remains the one to beat

Cut The Rope HD
Price: £1.19

Few games are as simple and as compelling as Cut The Rope. Each level has a piece of candy and Om Nom the monster. Using the objects in the level, you have to get the candy in Om Nom's mouth. Early levels begin with simple ropes and bubbles requiring a quick slice with your finger to cut the rope, later levels add fiendish complexity.

Rating: ★ ★ ★ ★ ★

Real Racing HD 2
Price: £5.99

One of the few games designed specifically to take advantage of the faster graphics chip in the iPad 2, the visuals in Real Racing 2 are the best way to show off what your new iPad 2 is capable of. Real Racing remains the benchmark for iOS gaming, bringing console quality graphics and gameplay to the small screen. Recommended.

Rating: ★ ★ ★ ★ ★

Angry Birds HD
Price: £2.99

The concept is simple; flick birds from a catapult and smash the green pigs. Angry Birds is a first-rate puzzler that makes excellent use of the iPad's touchscreen display. It's also one of the most fun games on the platform, with funny graphic touches and accessible gameplay. Every bit as addictive as the iPhone version, but better looking.

Rating: ★ ★ ★ ★ ★

Utilities

Pages

Price: £5.99

Apple's premier word-processing application enables you to create wonderfully designed documents, complete with images, tables, charts and all the formatting options you could dream of. And the templates are a joy to behold. The virtual keyboard can be frustrating, but combine this with a Keyboard Dock and you'll be typing faster.

Rating: ★ ★ ★ ★

Good Reader

Price: 59p

The iPad is an amazing book reader, there's just one problem. The iBooks app only displays ePub documents. Good Reader is a superb addition to iBooks that enables you to view other formats, including TXT, PDF, HTML, and Microsoft Office files. And at just 59p, it's an essential purchase for fans of reading eBooks on the go.

Rating: ★ ★ ★ ★ ★

BBC iPlayer

Price: Free

The BBC's flagship website needs no introduction. But whereas the iPhone accessed iPlayer through a mobile website, the iPad has a gorgeous app designed especially for it. The only downside is that you can't download programs to watch later and it only works via a WiFi connection. It's still an app every iPad owners should get.

Rating: ★ ★ ★ ★

The BBC's flagship website needs no introduction, but the iPad has a gorgeous iPlayer app

Things for iPad

Price: £11.99

We love Things. As the name suggests it takes all the things you have to do in your life, and crunches them into easily manageable projects. You can tag tasks into things you do at home, at work, at the shops, when you're bored. You can make tasks high priority, low priority, even have someday/maybe lists for things you really want to do one day. See page 154 for the full story.

Rating: ★ ★ ★ ★

Numbers

Price: £5.99

The undisputed star of Apple's iWork range is Numbers – something of a surprise, because it was hard to envisage how it would transfer to the iPad. While doing spreadsheets on the iPad might not sound the most fun, Numbers makes short work of number crunching. The virtual keyboard changes according to what is inside a cell (be it data, text, or a formula). It's certainly dry, but still very useful.

Rating: ★ ★ ★

Keynote

Price: £5.99

Keynote is the most powerful presentation software on the planet for Mac OS X. It's Apple at its very best. The iPad version is somewhat more of a challenge, but it's still useful for playing with and editing presentations on the move. You can create amazing presentations with your fingers – with cool transitions and animations – then use the iPad to show off your slides.

Rating: ★ ★ ★

Korg iElectribe

Price: £5.99

If you're into dance music, then you've probably spent some time listening to a Korg Electribe. This box provides a combination of synthesised music and drum machine, and creates many classic dance sounds. The Korg iElectribe recreates the famous box (dials and all) on the iPad and the multi-touch display enables you to twiddle and twirl your way to dance perfection.

Rating: ★★★★★

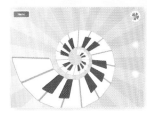

Magic Piano

Price: 59p

Some applications are hard to define, and magic piano is one of them. This app enables you to create piano music by tapping the screen. But rather than just display a traditional keyboard, the app uses several unique modes: such as one where glowing dots fall from the screen and have to be tapped; and another where a circular keyboard enables you to play.

Rating: ★★★★

GarageBand

Price: £5.99

Apple's legendary music-making program should be high on the shopping list for any iPad owner with an interest in music. You can connect your iPad to a musical instrument and record tracks in real time, or just bash virtual intruments on the screen. It's clever enough to even tell how hard you're tapping the drums. Great fun!

Rating: ★★★★★

Shazam for iPad

Price: Free

Shazam is an interesting app that listens to any audio and recognises the track. What started out as a party trick app has transformed into a music network with millions of users tagging and sharing audio info with music recommendations and charts. With data on over 8 million tracks Shazam is a great way to discover new music.

Rating: ★★★★

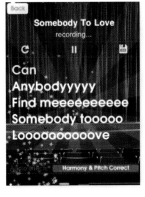

Glee

Price: 59p

For those that don't know, *Glee* is a sugar-coated American musical-comedy drama that is loved and loathed in equal measure. The app is wonderful though, because it combines karaoke with the same kind of technical wizardry used to make all bad singers sound good. As you sing it adjusts your voice and adds harmonising effects too. And you can even share your warblings on social networks – great party fun.

Rating: ★★★★★

Baby Decks DJ

Price: £14.99

This is a bold attempt to bring mixing deck performance to the iPad. Baby Decks DJ turns the iPad touch screen into a visual representation of two decks, cross fader, pitch control, and transformer bars. It's a great app for practicing mixing. The only downside is that it can't access music from the iTunes library – you have to upload tracks to it.

Rating: ★★★

Apple's legendary music-making program GarageBand should be high on the shopping list

Creativity & design

SketchBook Pro
Price: £4.99

Autodesk's SketchBook Pro is the best high-end painting and drawing app for the iPad. The iPad is very well suited to freeform sketching, but SketchBook Pro's strength is that it uses the same engine as the desktop version, and supports layers and multiple undo.

Rating: ★ ★ ★ ★

Adobe Ideas
Price: Free

Adobe Ideas is a free sketchbook app that turns your hand scribblings into curvaceous lines. It automatically straightens out curves, making everything look subtly nice. It's not as good as Brushes or SketchBook Pro for pure drawing, but great for jotting down ideas neatly.

Rating: ★ ★ ★ ★

Brushes
Price: 59p

This is another app that budding artists should consider. While it doesn't have as many options as ArtStudio or SketchBook Pro, it is perhaps the easiest and most fun way to doodle on the iPad, and is great for sketching over photographs. A great way to start digital drawing.

Rating: ★ ★ ★ ★

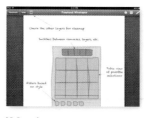

Photogene for iPad
Price: £2.39

There are a few different apps that enable you to make the most out of your images, and while none are like Photoshop on the desktop, plenty like Photogene offer a lot of professional editing tools including cropping, sharpening, colour adjustment and special effects.

Rating: ★ ★ ★ ★

iMovie
Price: £5.99

Few apps makes as much sense as iMovie on the iPad. Adding, cutting, and editing clips with your fingers is an instinctive and enjoyable experience. Adding effects and text is a bit clumsy though, but for all that this is a great showcase for what can be done on the iPad, and a must-have for any video buffs.

Rating: ★ ★ ★ ★

ArtStudio for iPad
Price: 59p

If you're into hand drawn art, then Art Studio is one of two apps you should consider (the other being Brushes). This app enables you to draw with a variety of different tools and there are some great options for layering images.

Rating: ★ ★ ★ ★

Sketchbook Pro's great strength is that it uses the same engine as the desktop version

Books & newspapers

iBooks

Price: Free

Apple's own electronic book reader is a must-download. This app enables you to purchase ebooks from the online iBookstore (including 30,000 free books – mostly classics so far). You can also add your own books that are in the ePub format (like MP3 for books). Flick from one page to the next and adjust text size and display font. If you turn it landscape you can see the whole spread. Reading has never been more fun.

Rating: ★★★★

The Elements: A Visual Exploration

Price: £7.99

With the arrival of the iPad, many publishers have started to rethink just how information should be presented. The Elements is the first eBook truly developed for the touchscreen iPad, and displays the elements that make up the periodic table. Where it gets clever is the animation that enables you to spin around objects, and the touch-screen navigation of the table.

Rating: ★★★★

BBC News

Price: Free

There's a calm serenity about BBC News that's lacking on other news organisations, and the BBC News app is a great way to view the day's stories. While we think it's a bit cluttered in horizontal mode, it's great in vertical mode and caches stories so you can read them offline. There's some doubt as to whether this app will be available on the UK store, due to concerns voiced by rival news organisations, but we'll soon find out.

Rating: ★★★

> With the arrival of the iPad, many publishers have started to rethink just how information should be presented

Wall Street Journal

Price: Free

It's a shame that most of the big newspapers on the iPad are American, but there's no doubting the quality of both this and the NYT app. You need to take out a subscription to read all the stories though, which at $3.99 a week is hardly cheap

Rating: ★★★

NYT Editors' Choice

Price: Free

The New York Times is a superb newspaper, even though like the Wall Street Journal it is largely focussed on the USA rather than worldwide. This great app features a daily selection of high-profile stories and makes for a great quick read.

Rating: ★★★★★

Guardian Eyewitness

Price: Free

While most news apps are busy rethinking a newspaper or website-based experience, *The Guardian* has taken a different tack. Its Guardian Eyewitness app makes use of the iPad's gorgeous display to present photographic pictures of the day. Each picture comes with a brief description, and professional photography tips. You get a real variety of modern news photography, and it's regularly stunning.

Rating: ★★★★★

iPad & iPhone User Subscribe today save 83%

Subscribe to iPhone & iPad User

Save a bundle and get each issue delivered straight to your door

● Pad & iPhone User regulars can get every issue delivered directly to their door and save 83% on the shop prices by taking out a subscription direct.

With an iPad & iPhone User subscription, you'll get the magazine delivered straight to your door, so you don't have to keep an eye out for copies at the newsagents. We also deliver the first run from the press direct to our subscribers, so they're always the first to get the latest information. And it's a great way to support your favourite magazine.

A subscription saves you money and makes sure you get your copy of iPad & iPhone User first

Subscribing to iPad & iPhone User:

We'll offer you the next three issues for just £1 each. And after that a six issue subscription to iPad & iPhone User will cost just £24.99.

Get all this

✓ Every issue delivered directly to your door

✓ Save 83 per cent off of the cover price

✓ Be the first to read each issue with priority delivery

Read on your iPad & iPhone

Digital Magazines
You can read all your favourite magazines on your iPad, iPhone, or on your computer. At the Zinio UK store you'll find digital versions of magazines like iPad & iPhone User, Macworld, and books like this Complete Guide To the iPad 2. Each title contains exactly the same material as appears in the print version. Get ready to join the digital revolution…
www.macworld.co.uk/zinio

App Store Apps
iPad & iPhone User has created a fantastic free app called AppWorld that enables you to read all its amazing reviews on your iPhone. The AppWorld app is packed with all the latest app reviews and enables you to get apps straight from the App Store. You'll never miss another great app again.
www.macworld.co.uk/appworld

and save 83%

Message from the editor

Here at iPad & iPhone User, we've been covering the world of Apple gadgets right from the word go.

So, whenever you read a copy of iPad & iPhone User, you can be sure you're getting the very sharpest insight into this exciting new world.

A subscription saves you money, and makes sure you get your copy before it's even in the shops.

So sign up for your regular insight into the most exciting gadgets in the world.

Mark Hattersley
mark_hattersley@idg.co.uk

Social network

We're a pretty social bunch here at iPad & iPhone User, and we love to chat to our readers. You can email us on inbox@ipadiphoneuser.co.uk or use any of these social networks…

inbox@ipadiphoneuser.co.uk

@ipadiphoneuser

www.facebook.com/ipadiphoneuser

www.ipadiphoneuser.co.uk

TERMS & CONDITIONS

- No obligation – we'll give you a full refund on any unmailed issues if you ever decide to cancel
- After three issues for £3, your iPad & iPhone User subscription will continue at the discounted rate of £24.99 for 6 issues
- For subscribers paying by cheque or credit card.

- subscription rate is £24.99 for 6 issue
- You'll receive 6 issues in a 12-month subscription
- Your subscription will start with the next available issue
- For overseas rates please call +44 1858 438 867 and quote reference CGi2

- For overseas rates please call +44 1858 438 867 and quote reference CGi2

Plug and play – setting up your iPad out of the box

Learn how to activate the iPad and sync it using iTunes

AFTER UNBOXING YOUR iPAD, YOU WILL NEED TO activate it using iTunes running on a desktop or laptop. If you haven't got a computer, Apple Stores should be willing to do the activation for you, but you're better off activating your iPad on your own PC or Mac, because you can then add content and apps from the computer.

The tutorial on page 46 walks you through the process of setting up an iPad. For now, the most important thing to note is that an iPad can only be linked to a single iTunes library, so link it with the computer you'll most often connect it to. Once you sync the iPad with another library, the content from the new library will replace the corresponding type of content already on the iPad, so you may want to proceed with care.

You'll notice that in the walkthrough, we don't recommend automatically syncing content during set-up. That's simply because doing so can take a very long time. We suggest that having activated your iPad, you then select specific content (iTunes playlists, individual films, certain iPhone apps) to add to it.

Note that when you first check 'Sync Apps', iTunes will try to add them all to your iPad, a process that may take several minutes. If you subsequently want to uncheck all apps, Command-click (Mac) or AltGr-click (Windows) any app in the sort list.

Finally, while you can fill your iPad to the brim, leave some space free (say 0.5–1GB), because without it larger apps may not update properly later on.

KIT LIST:
- iPad
- Desktop or laptop computer with iTunes 9.1 or later
- Internet connection

Time required: 10 mins
Difficulty: Beginner

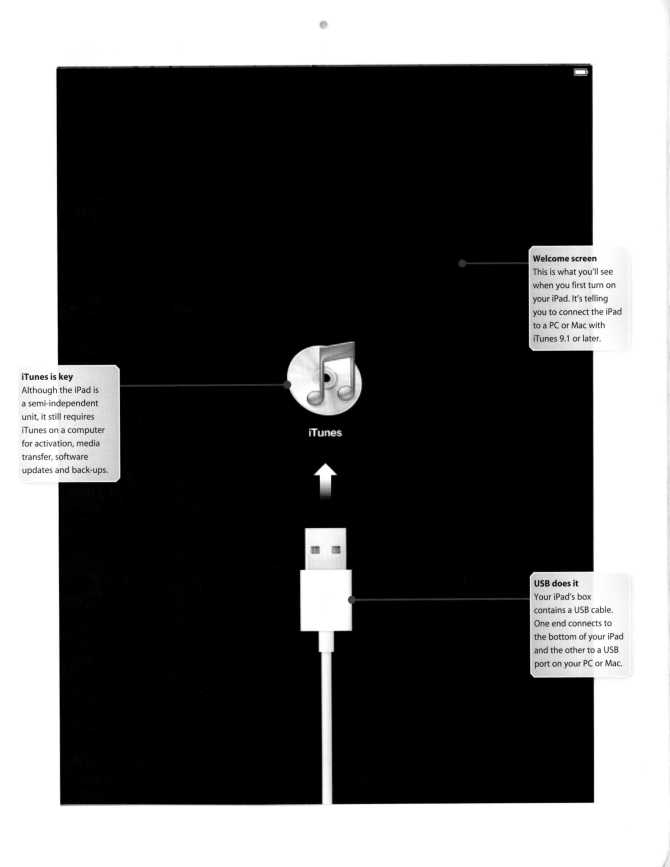

iTunes

Welcome screen
This is what you'll see when you first turn on your iPad. It's telling you to connect the iPad to a PC or Mac with iTunes 9.1 or later.

iTunes is key
Although the iPad is a semi-independent unit, it still requires iTunes on a computer for activation, media transfer, software updates and back-ups.

USB does it
Your iPad's box contains a USB cable. One end connects to the bottom of your iPad and the other to a USB port on your PC or Mac.

STEP BY STEP GUIDE: **iPad start-up**

1 Name your iPad Plug your iPad into your computer and you'll be asked to name it. Uncheck all of the checkboxes so you can manually define what to sync. Click 'Done'.

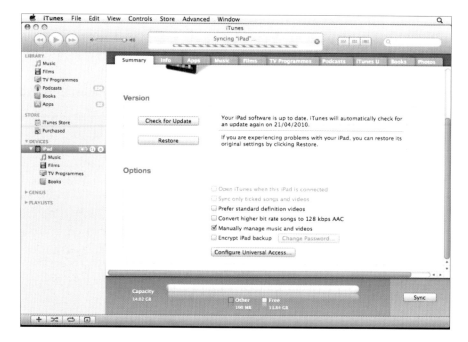

2 Do the initial sync Your iPad will sync with your library, to which it is now linked. Note the options in the Summary screen, including downsampling of audio ('Convert...') to save space on your iPad.

3 Sync content Tabs within iTunes provide access to different types of content. Select each in turn, tap the 'Sync' checkbox and define which playlists, apps, videos or photos you want to sync.

4 Start using your iPad Once your sync (or syncs) are done, your content is ready to use on your iPad. In the tutorials that follow, we show you how to use the preinstalled apps and download new ones.

Home screen

By default, your iPad's home screen gives access to 13 apps. These can't be deleted, but you can rearrange them by touching and holding any one until all the icons start jiggling; now drag and drop them as you see fit. Up to six apps can also be stored in the Dock below. To create an additional home screen, drag an app 'off-screen' to the right and it will appear on a new home screen.

Introducing Safari for iPad – the ultimate web browser

Learn how to use gestures and pages in Safari for iPad

AS WITH APPLE'S COMPUTERS AND iPHONES, Safari is the default web browser for the iPad – and on this platform it offers the best of both worlds. From the iPhone version, you get a gestural touch-based interface, with flick-scrolling, pinch-zooming and links that you activate by tapping them. With the large iPad screen, this gives you a truly effortless web-browsing experience that is also highly intuitive.

Another aspect of Safari for iPhone that benefits from extra screen space is the pages feature. Pages are similar to a desktop browser's tabs, enabling you to browse multiple sites simultaneously or send a link to a new page to read later.

However, Safari for iPad also borrows some ideas from its desktop cousin, notably a toolbar which sits permanently at the top of the screen, unlike on the iPhone where the toolbar sits at the bottom, with the address and search fields moving out of sight when you scroll a page.

The toolbar also houses the web page's title, which therefore remains on-screen at all times (unless you're viewing specific media content in full-screen, such as a video).

Here we show you how to get started with Safari, working with gestures, pages and web video. Once you start interacting directly with web content on the iPad's gorgeous screen, you'll be hooked. In fact, you may well find the combination of your computer's browser and a mouse starts to feel rather archaic by comparison.

KIT LIST:

■ **iPad**
■ **Internet connection**

Time required: 10 mins
Difficulty: Beginner

Search the web
The familiar search field occupies its customary spot in the top right of the toolbar – as it does on the iPhone and desktop versions of Safari.

Safari's toolbar
The toolbar buttons in Safari enable you to go back and forward, access the pages screen, go to your bookmarks, and bookmark a web page.

Standard websites
Unlike Safari for iPhone, the iPad version defaults to the standard version of a web page, not the mobile version, so you get a fuller experience.

STEP BY STEP GUIDE: Getting to know Safari for iPad

1 Open a web page... If you know the site you'd like to visit, tap the address field. When the keyboard appears, type the website's address and tap 'Go' to confirm, or select a site from your history.

2 ... Or search the web To search the web instead, tap the 'Google' field, type a search term, and tap 'Search'. Note: you can switch the search engine to Yahoo in the Safari section of the Settings app.

3 Navigate a page Drag to scroll; scroll bars appear briefly to show how much of a page you're viewing. Flick to scroll quickly in any direction.

4 Zoom page content Simply use spread and pinch gestures, or double-tap to zoom to a text column; a second double-tap reverts to full-screen.

5 Use pages Tap the pages icon in the toolbar, then tap a 'New Page' slot to open a new page. You can have up to nine pages open at once.

6 Handle links and images Tap-hold a link for more options. Tap-hold an online image and tap 'Save Image' to use it in the Photos app.

A good turn

Like Safari for iPhone, the iPad version works well in both portrait and landscape orientations. If you find yourself regularly zooming in and out on a certain website, try rotating your iPad to landscape mode – the page will resize accordingly, and the text will be bigger. Although you will then see less of the web page overall, the effortless scroll-based navigation of Safari for iPad means this is rarely, if ever, a problem.

7 Play video To start playing a video, tap the play icon at its centre and it will play inline. To access controls for play/pause and scrubbing through the clip, tap the video. Controls fade after a few seconds.

8 Go full-screen Tap the icon at the bottom right of a video and it will fill your display. Tap the video again to access controls. Tap 'Done' to return to the video's parent web page.

How to have fun with Photo Booth

Take twisted, wacky pictures with the iPad 2's built-in photo app

AS SHOULD NOW BE CLEAR, APPLE HAS ADDED TWO cameras to the iPad 2's feature set. It could have stopped there and just let you get on with it, but to add a splash of fun to proceedings and highlight how versatile they are, it's also installed this infectious little app as standard. No need to download Photo Booth from the App Store – it will be ready out of the box.

Compared to, say, iMovie's feature-heavy set-up, Photo Booth really is as simple as they come. Just point one of the iPad's cameras at your subject, choose one of eight wacky effects and snap away. You can take a picture of yourself in infrared or through an X-ray lens, create bizarre kaleidoscopic collages or twist a friend's face into all manner of crazy contortions. Then, once you've captured your madcap portrait, you can share it with friends at the tap of a button. Or, if you're that way inclined, store it on your camera roll for posterity and then threaten to upload it to Facebook next time you want something from the subject.

It's an extremely straightforward app to use so won't take more than a couple of minutes to get your head around. Read on to find out how it works.

KIT LIST:
- iPad 2
- A willing subject
- A wi-fi connection (for instant sharing)

Time required: 3-4 mins
Difficulty: Beginner

Say cheese!
As in the iPad or iPhone's standard camera app, just press this button to snap your picture, once you've got your subject lined up.

Picture preview
Compose your picture before you snap with the app's real-time preview display.

View your library
This strip displays all your most recent pictures. Just tap one to bring it up for closer viewing or to share with a friend.

Switch cameras
This button lets you switch between the self-portrait-friendly front-facing camera or, if you're shooting someone else, the back-facing lens.

Choose your effect
Hit the tab in the bottom left-hand corner of the screen to change the selected effect. There are eight different filters to choose from.

STEP BY STEP GUIDE: Taking pictures with Photo Booth

1 Choose your effect First things first, you need to choose which effect you want to inflict on your subject. The selection screen will be the first thing you see when you boot up the app, offering eight different filters to choose from.

2 Line up your shot Tapping on one of the available filters will take you to the shooting screen, detailed in full on page 53. The Thermal Camera displays heat signatures – perfect for recreating your favourite *Predator* set-piece.

3 X-Ray spectacle Don't worry, the X-Ray effect isn't able to show what sort of underwear you're sporting. Maybe Apple will add that in the next iOS update?

4 Kaleidoscope for improvement The Kaleidoscope filter lets you come up with some seriously out-there images. Not one for the family portrait but fun nevertheless.

5 Feeling the squeeze Okay, this is where the freak show really starts. The Squeeze effect pinches your face into all manner of ghastly contortions. Time to live out your E.T. fantasies.

6 Spinning around Twirl spins your face into a twisted, freakish vortex. This one is perfect for passport photos, driving licence snaps or any other official government ID.

Tweak the filters

While using the Mirror, Kaleidoscope, Light tunnel, Squeeze, Twirl or Stretch filters, you can move the 'focus point' of the effect by dragging it around the touch screen with your finger.

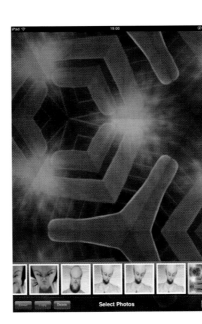

7 At a stretch Ever wondered what you'd look like if you had a fleshy cuboid for a head? Of course you have. The Stretch effect offers just that, pulling your face into a perfect square.

8 Share your images Once you've taken a picture, tap on it then press the 'Share' tab in the bottom-right corner. You can then email the image direct from the app, or copy it for further use.

How to: video chat with FaceTime

Make face-to-face phone calls with the iPad 2's twin cameras

AS WELL AS ALLOWING YOU TO SNAP PHOTOS AND capture video footage, the iPad 2's new twin cameras also add one more important feature to your tablet's toolkit – the ability to make video calls. With the new FaceTime app included on your device as standard, you can speak to friends and family face-to-face and free of charge via your internet connection.

This isn't the app's debut appearance – it was included as standard on the iPhone 4 from launch, while Mac users have been able to pick it up from the App Store since February this year. However, the newly optimised iPad 2 version is arguably the definitive iteration of the software, offering portable video calling on a big screen display.

It's very easy to use – all you have to do is create an Apple ID if you don't already have one, build an address book of your contacts and then start chatting. The person you want to call will also need to have an Apple ID, a compatible device (an iPad 2, iPod touch, iPhone 4 or Mac) and their own copy of FaceTime app but, aside from that, it couldn't be easier to use.

Over the next few pages we'll talk you through the basics of setting up an account, adding contacts and making calls. Time to say goodbye to those pricey phone bills...

KIT LIST:
- iPad 2
- A friend with a compatible Apple device
- A wi-fi connection (for instant sharing)
- An Apple ID

Time required: 5 mins
Difficulty: Beginner

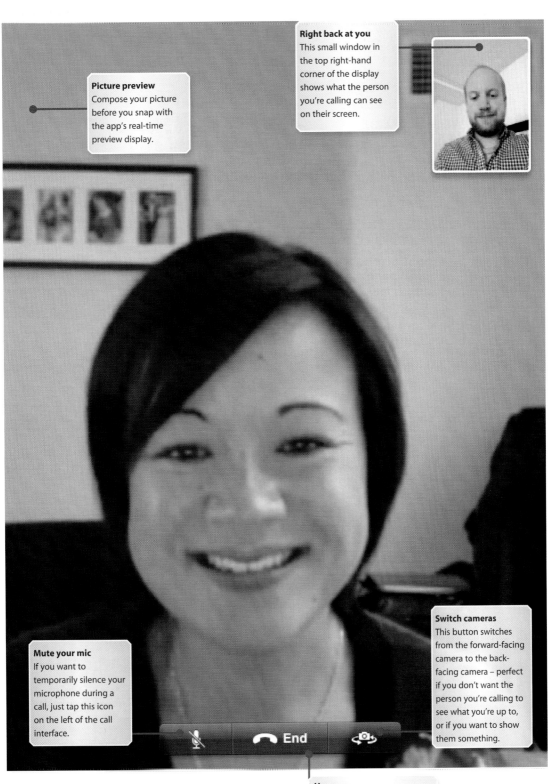

Picture preview
Compose your picture before you snap with the app's real-time preview display.

Right back at you
This small window in the top right-hand corner of the display shows what the person you're calling can see on their screen.

Switch cameras
This button switches from the forward-facing camera to the back-facing camera – perfect if you don't want the person you're calling to see what you're up to, or if you want to show them something.

Mute your mic
If you want to temporarily silence your microphone during a call, just tap this icon on the left of the call interface.

End

Hang up
Time to say goodbye? Just tap the 'End' button to hang up and bring your voice chat to a close.

STEP BY STEP GUIDE: Make video calls with FaceTime

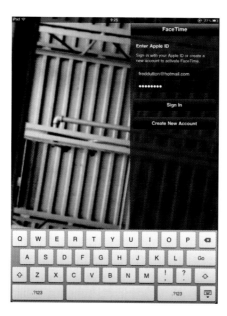

1 Signing in The first thing you'll need to do when you boot up the app is enter your Apple ID or, if you don't have one, create a new account. There's no cost involved and you'll need one in the future to pick up new apps, so don't hesitate.

2 Confirm your details Your contacts will track you down via your email address, so you need to verify which address you want FaceTime to use. To change the default address attached to your Apple ID just tap it and enter a new one.

3 Build your address book Before you can make any calls you'll need to enter contacts into your address book. Just tap the '+' in the top right-hand corner to get started.

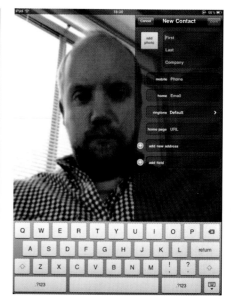

4 Creating a contact To add a contact fill in the form by tapping on the relevant field and typing in details. Make sure you include the email address, as this will be matched with an Apple ID.

5 Add to favourites Once you've entered a contact, you'll then be given the option of sharing a contact with a friend via email or adding it to your favourites list. This is just a convenient way of prioritising the people you call the most.

6 Make a call You're ready to make a call. Just tap a name in your address book and, providing they are kitted out with FaceTime, a call request will immediately be sent to them. If they're online and accept the call your voice chat will then begin.

7 Switching view As default, the front-facing camera will be on during a call so you can see each other. If you want to switch to the back-facing lens, just tap the camera switch icon

8 Receiving a call If a friend is trying to reach you, a box will pop up on your screen displaying their name. Hit the green 'Accept' tab to accept the call, or the red 'Decline' button to not.

Silent running

If you don't want to be disturbed by FaceTime calls while you're using your iPad you can temporarily disable the app. Tap the Settings icon on the home screen, go to the FaceTime tab and toggle FaceTime to 'Off'.

Reading and managing your email on the iPad

Find out how to read, write, delete and file your email

MAIL IS A GOOD-LOOKING iPAD APP, AND AS THE previous walkthrough shows, care has been taken to optimise the experience for portrait and landscape modes, and to ensure users generally have an efficient and effective way to read, write and manage email.

A few big features were not mentioned in that walkthrough, and so we'll go through those now. Perhaps the most important is Mail's search facility. In portrait mode, this is housed in the 'Inbox' pop-up; in landscape mode, it's in the sidebar. In either case, type a search term and use the buttons to restrict your search to 'From', 'To' or 'Subject' fields, or use 'All' to search all of them. Note that at the time of writing, iPad Mail does not allow you to search the content of email messages.

By default, the aforementioned inbox (either in pop-up or sidebar form) enables fast access to recent emails. To access other folders (such as Spam in Google Mail, or Drafts), tap the button at the top left labelled with the account's name. You then tap a folder to access its content.

When you're on an account page, there's one 'higher' level that you can reach by tapping the same button (which will be labelled 'Accounts'). This enables you to move from one email account to another. Users with many email accounts (home, work etc.) will probably find this method awkward and time-consuming, and the unified Inbox support now puts all your incoming mail from all your accounts in one place.

KIT LIST:

- ■ **iPad with one or more email accounts set up**
- ■ **Internet connection**

Time required: 10 mins
Difficulty: Beginner

From: Apple

To: mark_hattersley

iPad 2 is here.

25 March 2011 05:16   ⦿ Mark

Hide

The toolbar
The four icons on the right of the toolbar are for moving messages, deleting messages, replying and composing a new message.

Shop Online | Find a Store | 0800 048 0408

Link actions
As in Safari, tap-hold a link to bring up a pop-up dialog that enables you to open the link or copy it to the clipboard.

http://applev2.komtools.net/r.php?
D=http%3A%2F%2Fin...11_4701_version1

Open

Save Image

Copy

d 2

t's faster. And it's here.

Buy at the Apple Retail Store
Pick up your iPad from 5:00 pm today and we'll help you set it up before you leave the store

shipping and free engraving.

Buy now ▶   Find a store ▶

Advanced rendering
As with Mail for the Mac, the iPad version deals well with complex emails, happily displaying images and coloured text. You can pinch-zoom, too.

STEP BY STEP GUIDE: Exploring the Mail app

1 Read messages In portrait mode, Mail acts rather like a full-screen email reader. The toolbar arrows let you view the next and previous email.

2 See your inbox Just tap the 'Inbox' button. The current email is highlighted; blue dots indicate unread emails. To read a message, tap its preview.

3 Use landscape mode In landscape mode, Mail resembles a desktop email app. The sidebar shows your inbox, and the main area to the right houses a scrollable area for your selected message.

4 Manage email Tap 'Edit' to manage your email. Tap previews to select/deselect messages. Selected items are added to a pile. Tap 'Delete' to trash the pile or 'Move' to put the emails in a folder.

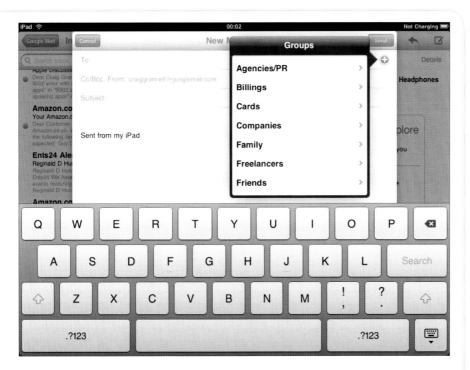

5 Compose a message Tap the icon at the top right to bring up the 'New Message' window, containing your default signature. You'll find typing easier in landscape mode, due to the larger keyboard.

6 Add contacts Tap the '+' icon to add recipients from the Contacts app, or tap the 'To' field and start typing to see a filtered list of matching contacts. Tap to select the one you want. Tap 'Send' to send.

Add a contact

Tap the name in the 'From' field of an email for a pop-up window with the sender's email address and other details. From this, you can create a new contact in the Contacts app by tapping 'Create New Contact' (the window expands, enabling you to add a photo and other details), or you can add the details to an existing contact by selecting them from the list that appears after you tap 'Add to Existing Contact'.

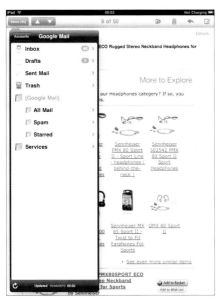

7 Save a draft If you tap 'Cancel', you can save a draft ('Save') in your Drafts folder. Tap the arrow with your account's name to access Drafts.

8 View attachments Images and PDFs will display inline; other attachments may open in apps. For more sophisticated PDF views, try GoodReader.

Watching films, TV shows, music videos and more

Getting to know the new Videos app

IF THERE'S ANY PROOF THAT WE'RE ALREADY living in the future, it's the fact that we have lightweight mobile devices that can store and play hours of video. Think about it: only 30 years ago, people had VHS decks that seemed to weigh about the same as a small horse and had gigantic keys. And just remembering the televisions of that era is enough to bring some of us out in a cold sweat.

Today, we have the iPad 2: 600 grams of portable goodness that can play back 10 hours of video on its spectacular screen before it needs recharging. And thanks to the fabulous Videos app, you have a great way to enjoy content you've downloaded from the iTunes store.

Now, it's true that quite a few people have claimed that the iPad is rubbish for video. Their argument is largely based on the fact that the iPad screen uses the 4:3 aspect ratio of older television sets, rather than widescreen. But this was a considered decision by Apple, and the dimensions were chosen as they are better for most content.

Sure, this means widescreen movies are 'letterboxed' by default (with black borders above and below), but the iPad's screen is big enough to enable you to comfortably enjoy your favourite shows while curled up on the couch or winging your way by plane to a holiday destination.

In this tutorial we show how Apple got mobile video right with its great new Videos app.

KIT LIST:

■ **iPad with some videos synced**

Time required: 10 mins
Difficulty: Beginner

Scrub bar
Jump rapidly to any point in a video clip with this handy control.

Video playback
Simplicity is key in the Videos app. The screen is normally black, apart from the video, but a tap brings up straightforward controls.

Remember your place
For videos you've watched part-way through, a small round indicator on the screen shows how much of the clip you've seen.

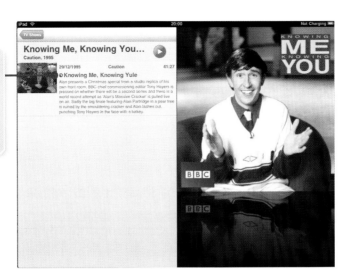

STEP BY STEP GUIDE: Exploring the Videos app

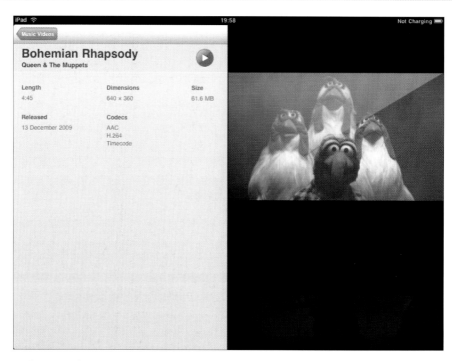

1 Choose what to watch The Videos app displays tabs in its top toolbar that group the clips on your iPad by category (for example, 'Music Videos'). Select one to see what is available to watch.

2 View video details Tap a video to zoom its artwork and also view more information about it. For films, you can switch between 'Info' and 'Chapters' via two toolbar buttons.

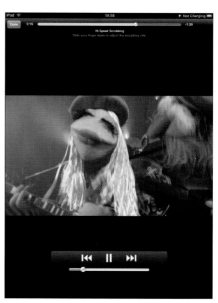

3 Start watching Just tap the play button to the right of the video's title. In portrait mode, the video will sit halfway up the screen.

4 Use controls Tap the video to see the scrubbing bar (top), which lets you scan quickly through, plus play, pause, skip and volume buttons.

5 Go wide screen Rotate into landscape mode and the video fills more of the screen. Since the iPad has a 4:3 screen ratio, widescreen videos play 'letterboxed' – with black borders above and below.

6 Toggle video modes Using the button at the top right of the screen, you can toggle landscape video between letterboxed mode (the default) or full-screen but with the sides chopped off.

7 Watch on a real TV In the Settings app, select 'Video' to set options (widescreen and PAL/NTSC) for sending video from the iPad to a TV.

8 Set play options The 'Start Playing' menu has two self-explanatory options: 'Where Left Off' and 'From Beginning'.

Screen lock

You know how it is when you're watching a truly great piece of television or a wonderful movie – you simply don't want anything to distract you. You can stop one potential distraction on your iPad: once it's in landscape mode, activate the screen rotation lock (located on the side of the iPad, above the volume rocker switch). This will stop the video suddenly rotating should you happen to shift the iPad while you're watching.

Playing tunes and podcasts with the iPod app

Browse and play back your favourite music from your iPad

WHEN STEVE JOBS FIRST DEMOED THE iPAD, HE talked of how it sat between desktop and mobile devices. Appropriately enough, then, the iPod app for iPad is an app that sits halfway between iTunes for desktop computers and the iPod app for the iPhone.

The interface is definitely reminiscent of iTunes, to the point that it feels like a version of the desktop app streamlined purely for playing audio. The toolbar provides touch – and drag-based controls, and the sidebar gives access to your audio collection. To the right, your music (or podcasts and audiobooks) are listed, and you can choose from a number of different views.

The iPad version of the iPod app also borrows some tricks from the iPhone version, most notably, tracklistings in album view which spin into place – a feature that's both beautiful and usable. Importantly, the app also retains the iPhone version's ability to play in the background while you use other apps. All you need to do is start playing some music, close the iPod app, and launch something else. At any point, double-clicking the Home button should bring up a dialog with information about the currently playing track, playback controls (back, play/pause, forward and a volume slider), a 'Close' button and an 'iPod' button to launch the iPod app.

Usefully, iPod for iPad also provides features that enable you to create playlists and rapidly build automated tracklistings via Apple's Genius technology. There's more on these features in the tutorial after this one.

KIT LIST:

■ iPad with some music or podcasts

Time required: 10 mins
Difficulty: Beginner

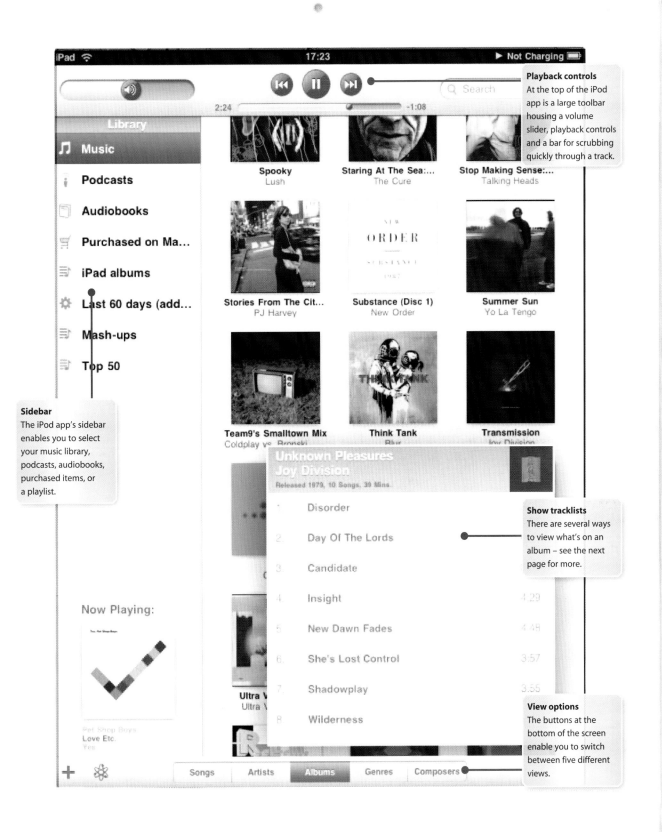

iPad 🔊   17:23   ▶ Not Charging 🔋

2:24   -1:08

🔍 Search

Library

🎵 Music

▌ Podcasts

▢ Audiobooks

🛒 Purchased on Ma...

☰ iPad albums

⚙ Last 60 days (add...

☰ Mash-ups

☰ Top 50

Spooky
Lush

Staring At The Sea:...
The Cure

Stop Making Sense:...
Talking Heads

Stories From The Cit...
PJ Harvey

ORDER

Substance (Disc 1)
New Order

Summer Sun
Yo La Tengo

THINK TANK

Team9's Smalltown Mix
Coldplay vs. Bronski

Think Tank
Blur

Transmission
Joy Division

Now Playing:

✓

Pet Shop Boys
Love Etc.
Yes

Unknown Pleasures
Joy Division
Released 1979, 10 Songs, 39 Mins.

1.	Disorder	
2.	Day Of The Lords	
3.	Candidate	
4.	Insight	4:29
5.	New Dawn Fades	4:48
6.	She's Lost Control	3:57
7.	Shadowplay	3:55
8.	Wilderness	

Ultra V
Ultra V

+ ⚛

Songs   Artists   **Albums**   Genres   Composers

Playback controls
At the top of the iPod app is a large toolbar housing a volume slider, playback controls and a bar for scrubbing quickly through a track.

Sidebar
The iPod app's sidebar enables you to select your music library, podcasts, audiobooks, purchased items, or a playlist.

Show tracklists
There are several ways to view what's on an album – see the next page for more.

View options
The buttons at the bottom of the screen enable you to switch between five different views.

STEP BY STEP GUIDE: Browsing and playing music

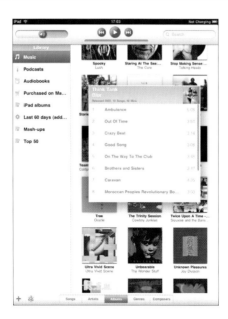

1 View your albums In the iTunes-like view, tap 'Albums' to view a scrollable list of albums in alphabetical order. Tap an album to bring up a tracklist window (which can also be scrolled).

2 Play a track Tap a track to play it and view full-screen cover art. Tap the artwork to bring up various controls, including a scrub bar. The button in the bottom right shows the full album tracklist.

3 Rate tracks While viewing the album tracks, you can rate the current song by tapping a rating dot. Tap the cover (bottom right) for the previous screen, or the left-arrow for the iTunes-like view.

4 Songs view Tap 'Songs' to see an alphabetical list of the songs on your iPad. Tap a letter at the right-hand side to 'snap' to a group of tracks starting with that letter.

5 Artists view Tap 'Artists' to view your albums, grouped by performer. Select an artist and 'Play All Songs' to play all tracks by that artist, or tap a track to play an album from that point on.

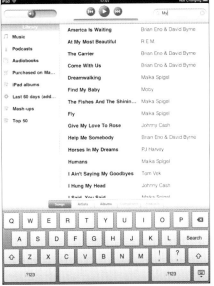

6 Search for songs Whichever view you're in, available items can be filtered by typing in the search field. Note that in songs view, the matches displayed could be for artist, album or song.

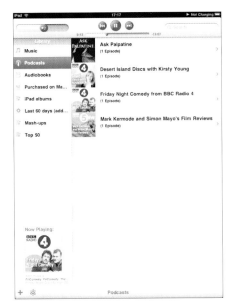

7 Play podcasts The iPod app lists all podcasts on your iPad, but it only plays audio ones (via a tap, just like a song). Tap a video podcast and it will open in the Videos app.

8 Need to recap? If the podcast isn't in full-screen mode, tap the art at the bottom left, then tap the full-screen art. You can now use a useful 'back 30 seconds' control at the bottom.

Go full-screen
Full-screen mode gives access to a number of controls not present in the more iTunes-like iPod app views. For standard songs, you will see 'repeat' and 'shuffle' controls positioned either side of the scrubbing bar. For podcasts, you get an email icon in the top left to tell someone about the podcast, and a speed control (which cycles between half-, regular- or double-speed playback) on the right.

How to: make music with GarageBand

Compose and record your own mini-masterpiece with Apple's portable home studio app

OF ALL THE NEW OR OPTIMISED APPS AVAILABLE for iPad 2 none are quite so fully-featured, fun to use and downright impressive as GarageBand, a new portable version of Apple's acclaimed Mac music studio software.

The app lets you record your own songs from scratch, either by plugging in your own instruments or using the digital versions provided. You can use up to eight separate audio tracks to build your composition and a range of features to fine tune it to perfection.

While the original Mac version has many ardent followers, this one arguably goes one step further than its home computing cousin. Not only does it pack in almost all the same editing features but, by adding digital guitars, bass, keyboards and drums, it's a much more versatile, hands-on experience too.

And on top of that, the 'smart' versions of those instruments that are offered really level the playing field, performing the hard work of smoothly playing an instrument for you while you concentrate on chord changes and special audio effects. This new feature gives users free rein to craft their own pocket symphonies, regardless of whether they're a complete beginner or an experienced musician. Take all that into account and, at only £2.99, you've got one of the very best deals on the App Store.

It would be impossible to cover everything GarageBand has to offer in just a few short pages but read on for our beginner's guide to getting set up and recording your first song.

KIT LIST:

- iPad 2
- **Guitar connector cable (if recording live instruments)**
- **A WI-Fi connection (for instant sharing)**

Time required: 30 mins
Difficulty: Intermediate/ Advanced

Strike a chord
Here's just one of the built-in digital instruments available: the Hard Rock guitar. To strum a chord, just tap the key name or stroke the strings. The app automatically groups chords that are in the same key, so that they work together in a song.

Autoplay it safe
Not much of a musician? Select one of the four Autoplay settings and let the app pick or strum rhythms or arpeggios for you while you just time the chord changes.

String theory
You can also pluck a single string by tapping it. If you hit the button in the top-right corner, the display will switch away from chords into a standard guitar view, letting you bend and hammer on or off notes, as well.

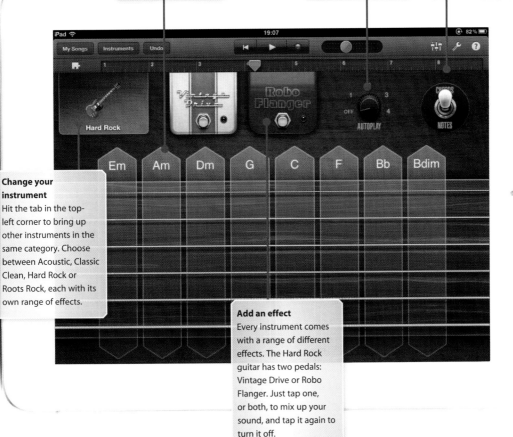

Change your instrument
Hit the tab in the top-left corner to bring up other instruments in the same category. Choose between Acoustic, Classic Clean, Hard Rock or Roots Rock, each with its own range of effects.

Add an effect
Every instrument comes with a range of different effects. The Hard Rock guitar has two pedals: Vintage Drive or Robo Flanger. Just tap one, or both, to mix up your sound, and tap it again to turn it off.

1 Pick your instrument The first thing you'll need to do when booting up the app is select an instrument to get started with. Take your pick from keyboards, guitar, bass and drums. You can also plug in your own live instrument, too, using a guitar cable connector (available seprately).

2 Lay down a rhythm Drums are always a good place to start. Hit the red 'Record' button at the top of the screen and then tap out your rhythm using the on-screen drum pads. The harder you tap the drums, the louder they'll sound.

3 Add another track Hit the tab at the top of the screen with three horizontal lines on it to bring up your studio view. This is where you'll manage your recording and add extra tracks. To add a second instrument tap the '+' in the bottom-left corner and make your selection.

4 Bring in the guitar Next up, some guitar. Hit the record button and pick or strum your tune. The drum track you record will play over the top so you can stick to the beat.

5 Time for some keys Repeat step three, but this time select keyboards. As with guitars, there are rang of different instruments to choose from, from grand piano to sci-fi synths, and a smart keyboard option that plays for you. Hit record, lay down your melody and head back to the studio screen.

6 Edit your track Once you've added all the instruments you want (up to eight), it's time to fine tune your creation. Drag the slider on the left of the screen out to tweak the volume of each different track.

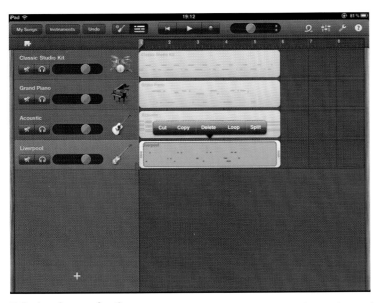

7 Strive for perfection To crop the length of tracks, just tap on them and move the slider left or right. You can pinch the screen to zoom in closer for more accurate editing. Double-tap to bring up a menu that lets you copy, delete, loop or split a track.

8 Share your song When you've finished, tap the 'My songs' tab. You can name your tune, email it to a friend or upload it to iTunes, after tapping the button shaped like a box with an arrow coming out of it.

Hot Tip

GarageBand also lets you plug in your own axe via a guitar connector cable (available separately). Not only that, but it offers then different pedals and 32 distinct amp types with which you can customise your sounds. There's even a built-in tuner!

Buying content from the iTunes Store

Get music, movies, TV shows, podcasts and audiobooks from the smartest online store in the world

ON A MAC OR PC, iTUNES IS THE SOFTWARE YOU USE as a media manager and to access the iTunes Store. On your iPad, just like on an iPhone or iPod touch, the iTunes app is essentially a front-end to the iTunes Store, with the iPod and Videos apps handling music and video playback respectively.

We rather like this separation of functionality on the iPad. The desktop iTunes application, especially the Windows version, has a tendency to feel bloated as it has to do so much. By contrast, iTunes for iPad is a joy – sleek, efficient, surprisingly tactile and a fun way to buy digital media.

There is, however, one odd quirk we've not noted elsewhere: in the 'New and Noteworthy' boxes, you might think you can access subsequent pages via a swipe, but you can't – instead, you must tap the arrows to move the 'carousel' in the direction of your choosing.

The following guided tour shows what's available in the iTunes app, and details how to search for, preview and download content. You will need an iTunes Store account for downloading to work.

If you don't already have an account, you can create one in a few minutes on your iPad by scrolling down to the bottom of any of the section pages, tapping 'Sign In', tapping 'Create New Account' in the pop-up dialog, and then adding the relevant info in the 'New Account' pop-up. It's definitely worth the (extremely minor) effort.

KIT LIST:

- iPad
- Internet connection
- An iTunes Store account

Time required: 10 mins
Difficulty: Beginner

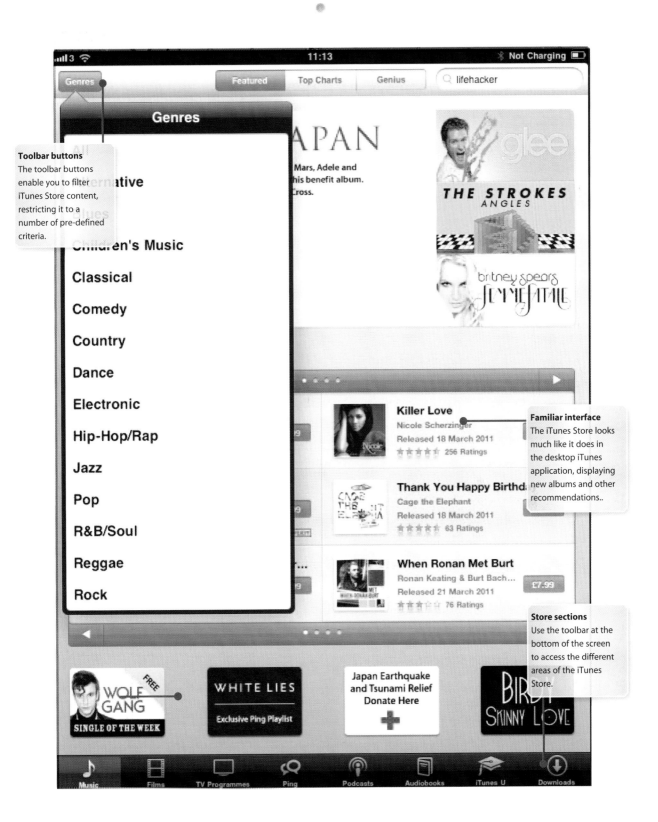

11:13   Not Charging

Genres   Featured   Top Charts   Genius   🔍 lifehacker

Genres

All
Alternative
Blues
Children's Music
Classical
Comedy
Country
Dance
Electronic
Hip-Hop/Rap
Jazz
Pop
R&B/Soul
Reggae
Rock

Toolbar buttons
The toolbar buttons enable you to filter iTunes Store content, restricting it to a number of pre-defined criteria.

...APAN

...Mars, Adele and ...his benefit album. ...Cross.

Killer Love
Nicole Scherzinger
Released 18 March 2011
★★★★☆ 256 Ratings

Thank You Happy Birthd...
Cage the Elephant
Released 18 March 2011
★★★★☆ 63 Ratings

When Ronan Met Burt
Ronan Keating & Burt Bach...
Released 21 March 2011   £7.99
★★★☆☆ 76 Ratings

Familiar interface
The iTunes Store looks much like it does in the desktop iTunes application, displaying new albums and other recommendations..

Store sections
Use the toolbar at the bottom of the screen to access the different areas of the iTunes Store.

WOLF GANG — FREE — SINGLE OF THE WEEK

WHITE LIES — Exclusive Ping Playlist

Japan Earthquake and Tsunami Relief Donate Here ✚

BIRDY SKINNY LOVE

♪ Music   Films   TV Programmes   Ping   Podcasts   Audiobooks   iTunes U   Downloads

STEP BY STEP GUIDE: **Buying from the iTunes Store**

1 Account details Scroll to the bottom of the page to see the name and credit for the signed-in account. Switch accounts by tapping 'Account', signing out and signing in with other details.

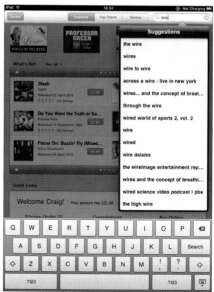

2 Search for content You can browse iTunes by tapping on-screen content, but to quickly find something, use the search field (which provides matches that update as you type).

3 Preview music Tap an album to view its details, and tap tracks for previews. Below will be ratings and related recommendations. Tap outside the window to close it.

4 Check out recommendations Tap an '... Also Bought' item and it pushes to the left what you were looking at, so you can preview the related item. Swipe it right to see the original window.

5 Preview videos Tap a video to see its details, and tap 'preview' to watch a snippet. Note: for TV series there may be a preview for each episode, as shown above. Tap a play icon to view.

6 Buy and download To buy something from iTunes, tap the relevant price button twice. A password dialog pop-up will appear. To go ahead, type in your password and tap 'OK'.

Shop around

iTunes for iPad is so elegant and inviting that it's easy to get carried away and download a ton of content from the iTunes Store. But note that the iPad can play content from a number of sources (for example, digital music from the likes of Amazon and Play, and other vendors), so it certainly pays to shop around. You can also play music you've ripped from your CD collection using iTunes for Mac or Windows.

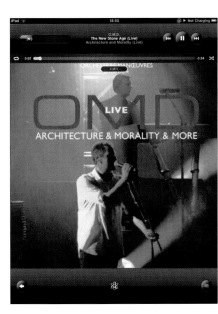

7 Track downloads To check the progress of your downloads, tap 'Downloads' on the bottom toolbar. Downloads can be paused if you need bandwidth to access other content.

8 Play your content For music, the 'Purchased' toolbar button closes iTunes and opens the 'Purchased' playlist in the iPod app, giving easy access to your newly downloaded tunes.

Find fantastic apps on the iPad App Store

Learn how to search the App Store for the best apps

 **ALTHOUGH APPLE'S iPHONE AND iPOD TOUCH ARE** terrific, boasting lovely touchscreen controls and a great interface, it's pretty clear that the App Store is also key to setting Apple devices apart from the competition. With the tens of thousands of apps and games now available, it's funny to realise that the App Store didn't actually exist when the iPhone was launched.

For the iPad, there is no such issue: iPhone and iPod touch apps are generally iPad-compatible, meaning loads of great products were available before the iPad even launched. Now developers are increasingly taking advantage of the iPad's larger screen and extra power, creating apps specifically for the device.

Because of this, the iPad's App Store application isn't the general front-end you see in the desktop version of iTunes, but instead prioritises iPad-optimised products (iPhone apps are available, too, though some may not work so well on the iPad, so remember to check app compatibility). Already, great products for business, making music, editing photos, social networking, productivity, reading news and even healthcare tasks are available, along with dozens of top-quality games to rival anything on competing platforms.

The App Store app itself generally works in a similar fashion to the iTunes App Store, although as our guided tour shows, the way you access categories can work somewhat differently. The carousels behave identically, though – they require arrows to be tapped, and don't respond to swipes left or right.

KIT LIST:

■ **iPad**
■ **Internet connection**
■ **iTunes Store account**

Time required: 10 mins
Difficulty: Beginner

iPad 📶   17:33   🔒 Not Charging 🔋

New   What's Hot   Q Search

App hunter
The Search field sits in the top toolbar, giving you rapid access to your favourite apps.

In the Spotlight

In the Spotlight
Featured and category pages showcase highlighted apps via a Cover Flow-style drag-based interface.

abcNotes - Sticky Notes for your iPad - Prod...

What's Hot   See All >

◄   • • • •   ►

Bowls HD - Authentic Tibetan...
Music
Released Mar 31, 2010
⭐⭐⭐⭐⭐ 11 Ratings
$3.99

Accordéon
Music
Released Apr 01, 2010
⭐⭐⭐⭐⭐ 12 Ratings
$2.99

Wikipanion Plus for iPad
Reference
Released Apr 01, 2010
⭐⭐⭐⭐⭐ 5 Ratings
$4.99

Drink-a-Dex
Reference
Released Apr 03, 2010
⭐⭐⭐⭐⭐ 8 Ratings
$1.99

The World Factbook for iPad
Reference
Released Apr 01, 2010
⭐⭐⭐⭐⭐ 8 Ratings
$1.99

Air Harp
Music
Released Apr 01, 2010
⭐⭐⭐⭐⭐ 9 Ratings
$1.99

◄   • • • •   ►

⊕ indicates an app designed for both iPhone and iPad

MAGIC PIANO   iWork f

YAHOO!

Featured   Top Charts   Categories   Updates

The main toolbar
Use the toolbar to switch between featured apps, the app charts and specific app categories.

STEP BY STEP GUIDE: Finding the best apps

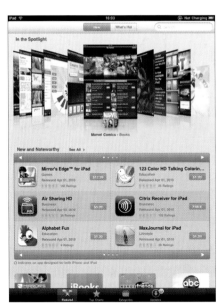

1 See the latest and greatest Tap the 'Featured' tab to access new apps (via the 'New' button) and apps Apple highly regards (via 'What's Hot'). Highlights also appear in ad-like buttons.

2 Check out staff picks In the 'New' page, scroll to 'Staff Favorites' and tap 'See All' for a page with loads more apps Apple likes. Tap 'Featured' to sort the list by name, release date or 'featured'.

3 Into the charts To see what other people are buying, tap 'Top Charts' in the toolbar. Top paid and free apps are shown in columns, with top-grossing products underneath.

4 See bestsellers by category Tapping the 'Categories' button and making a selection brings you the charts for that category. You can see past the top ten by tapping 'Show More' below.

5 Browse by category If you just tap the 'Categories' button, you'll see an overview of App Store categories with example apps. Tap one to see a category-specific page like the one from step 1.

6 View an app Tap an app's icon to visit its page. Tap 'Tell a Friend' to create a Mail message with a link to the app's store page. To view an app's full description, tap 'More'.

More info

While the App Store usually offers plenty of information about each app, you may sometimes want to find out more about features or exactly how the app will work. On the left of any App Store product page you should see 'Developer Web Site' and 'App Support' buttons. Tap one to launch Safari, which will take you to the relevant pages assigned by the developer.

7 See more screen grabs In landscape mode you can see the edge of the next screen grab for the app, but this isn't the case in portrait mode. Swipe grabs left and right to view more.

8 Read reviews Scroll down for customer opinions of the app (covering the current version only, unless you use the 'All Versions' button). Sort reviews (helpful/recent) with the 'Sort By' button.

How to direct your own film with iMovie

Edit your footage into the ultimate home movie with Apple's film studio

AS MANY MAC AND IPHONE 4 OWNERS WILL ALREADY know, iMovie is an intuitive, accessible piece of software that lets you edit together your digital video footage into a single film. With the addition of twin cameras to the iPad 2 Apple has now made the experience available for tablet users too.

Like it's progenitors, the portable version lets you splice together footage filmed with your iPad, or on another compatible Apple device, into a slick, professional movie. You can add in still images from your camera, add a soundtrack, record a voiceover and create your own credit sequence or title screens too. When you're done, you can then share your creation with friends or even upload to iTunes for the world to see.

This is a complete package, not just a scaled down taster of the full Mac experience. With the tablet's tactile touch screen controls and large display, it's actually easier to use than the smartphone version and more portable than the desktop original. At £2.99 it's hard to overstress just what great value iMovie is. Just try and find software anywhere near as fully-featured on a PC for ten times that amount.

Like GarageBand, iMovie is absolutely packed with knobs to tweak and dials to twirl so will take a little time to get your head around. Fear not though, with help from our step-by-step tutorial you'll be piecing together homespun blockbusters worthy of the big screen in no time.

KIT LIST:
- iPad 2
- iMovie app (£2.99)

Time required: 30 mins
Difficulty: Intermediate/Advanced

Your video clips
All of your raw video footage is displayed in this window. To drop it into your movie, just tap on it, pinch to select the desired frames then hit the arrow-shaped button and it will be placed in front of the scroller in your timeline.

Capture new footage
If you need to record more footage on the fly, there's no need to exit iMovie and bring up the standard camera app. Just hit this tab and start filming. Once you're done, the clip will immediately be added to your video library.

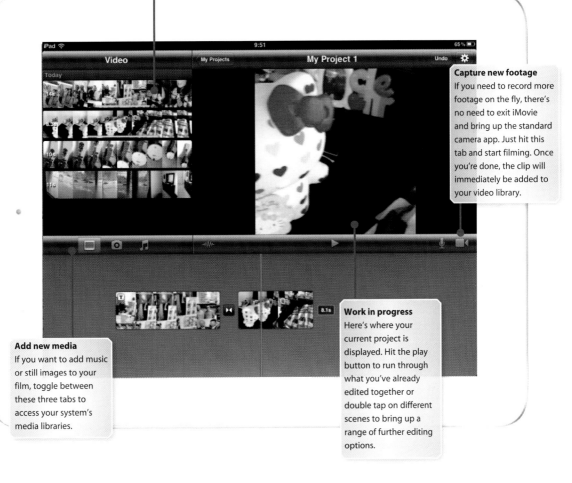

Add new media
If you want to add music or still images to your film, toggle between these three tabs to access your system's media libraries.

Work in progress
Here's where your current project is displayed. Hit the play button to run through what you've already edited together or double tap on different scenes to bring up a range of further editing options.

STEP BY STEP GUIDE: Making your first movie

1 Film some footage Boot up the iPad's built-in Camera app and capture your footage. You can switch between still camera and video capture using the switch on the bottom-right of the screen.

2 Getting started This is the first screen you'll be presented with when you start iMovie. Hit the '+' button to start a new project. You can also play and share any existing movies you've made.

3 Choose your first frames To insert frames, select the clip from the footage library on the left of the screen, pinch to zoom in on desired frames and tap the arrow-shaped button to drop it in.

4 Piece your film together
Add more clips as desired to slowly put your movie together. You can reposition clips by tapping and holding down on a segment and then dragging it to the desired place on the timeline, or crop their length.

5 Add an intro iMovie also lets you add a title screen or end credits to your film. Double-tap on your movie's first frame, select 'Title Style', then press 'Opening' and type in the text you'd like to appear. You can select a font theme by hitting the cog-shaped button in the top-right corner of the screen (see 'Fine tuning' panel).

6 Compose your soundtrack To add a soundtrack to your creation press the 'Music' button on the left of the screen. You can then pick a song from iTunes or add Sound Effects.

7 Find an audience All done? Hit the 'My Projects' button to return to the menu screen where you can name your film, play it full screen or share it with friends via email or by uploading it onto iTunes.

Record a voiceover

Should you want to record additional sound or add a voiceover, just hit the microphone button on the right of the screen and say your piece. Once you're done, you'll find the clip under the sounds tab on the left of the screen.

Seeing your appointments in the Calendar app

Learn about different views, searching for events, and more...

Tuesday

9

WITHOUT QUESTION, THE CALENDAR APP IS ONE of the biggest iPad app wins. The interface is clearly based on a real-world desktop calendar, and the result feels entirely natural and right rather than clichéd or tacky. The app has a surprisingly tactile feel, given that you interact with it by prodding and swiping at a piece of glass. It's one of the iPad's features that you really could use in isolation, without the help of a desktop computer.

Of course, it helps that the Calendar app is pretty capable. It doesn't quite offer the range of options found in the likes of iCal for Mac OS X, but it comes close. You get a bunch of different views (explored in full overleaf), enabling you to view your upcoming events in a number of ways. There's built-in search for quickly finding events that you can't see in the current view. And, as you'd expect, you can edit and create events directly on your iPad, rather than having to do so in your desktop application prior to a sync. How to work with events is detailed in the next tutorial.

You may also find the Calendar app highly beneficial even when you're office-bound. Put your iPad in a dock, perhaps set next to your computer, and turn off the auto-lock feature (via the 'Auto-Lock' menu within the 'General' section of the Settings app). This gives you a fantastic interactive calendar that also happens to look great. It certainly beats scribbling on a piece of paper with a marker pen.

KIT LIST:
- iPad
- A busy shedule in your Calendar

Time required: 10 mins
Difficulty: Beginner

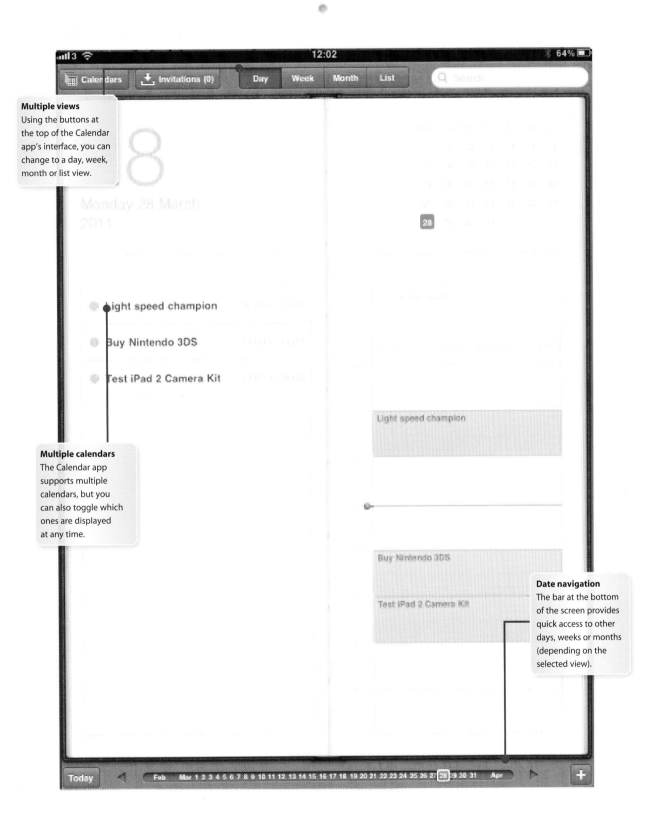

Multiple views
Using the buttons at the top of the Calendar app's interface, you can change to a day, week, month or list view.

Multiple calendars
The Calendar app supports multiple calendars, but you can also toggle which ones are displayed at any time.

Date navigation
The bar at the bottom of the screen provides quick access to other days, weeks or months (depending on the selected view).

STEP BY STEP GUIDE: **Navigating your calendars**

1 Day view In day view, the screen is split between a scrollable list of events and a day planner. Tap an event in either half of the screen to access the 'Edit Event' pop-up.

2 Navigate days Drag your finger along the date bar to select a different date. Lift your finger off the screen to confirm your choice. You can also tap the arrows to move day by day.

3 Week and month views The week and month views show events for a selected week or month. In either case, tap an event for a summary.

4 List view Tap the 'List' button to see, on the left, a column listing all upcoming events, grouped by day.

5 Toggle calendars Tap the 'Calendars' button to view the calendars you added during your most recent iTunes sync. Tap to toggle each on and off, or tap 'All' to turn all calendars on or off.

6 Snap to today If you've been adding and viewing events for upcoming days, weeks or months, you needn't manually navigate back to the current day's events – just tap the 'Today' button.

7 Search for events Use the search field to access a dynamically filtered list of events, grouped by day.

8 On the road? In the Settings app, hit 'Mail, Contacts, Calendars'. Turn off Time Zone Support and the time will be set according to your location.

Today's date?

Although the iPad lock screen shows the current date below the time, the date isn't shown when you navigate your home screens – only the time appears, at the top of the screen. However, the Calendar app's icon shows the current day and date. Put it in your dock and you'll be able to see the date at all times.

Adding and editing events in the Calendar app

Define locations, times, alerts and notes for events

Tuesday

9

APPLE PITCHES THE iPAD AS A DEVICE THAT inhabits a space between a smartphone and a laptop. With that in mind, it's conceivable that many iPad owners will use it, in part, as a gigantic PDA.

It therefore comes as no surprise that the iPad's Calendar app isn't entirely reliant on data sent to it via a sync – you can use it to add new events and also to amend existing ones. On a subsequent sync you can allow this updated data to overwrite the corresponding events on your desktop or laptop.

The process for adding a new event from scratch is pretty straightforward, but when it comes to editing events, it's worth noting one of the options in the 'Mail, Contacts, Calendars' section of the Settings app. Scroll down to 'Calendars' and you'll find the 'Default Calendar' option. Tap this to see a list of the calendars on your iPad. Select one of them and it will be used as the default in the Calendars app when you create a new event. The setting can be overridden on a per-event basis, but it's a good time-saver to have your most-used calendar as the default option.

You'll find that all of the screen grabs in this tutorial are in portrait mode. This is actually the best orientation for your iPad when you are creating new events, because it provides more vertical space for the 'Add Event' pop-up. This gives you a fuller overview and means you don't have to scroll to view the pop-up's content.

KIT LIST:

■ **iPad**

Time required: 10 mins
Difficulty: Beginner

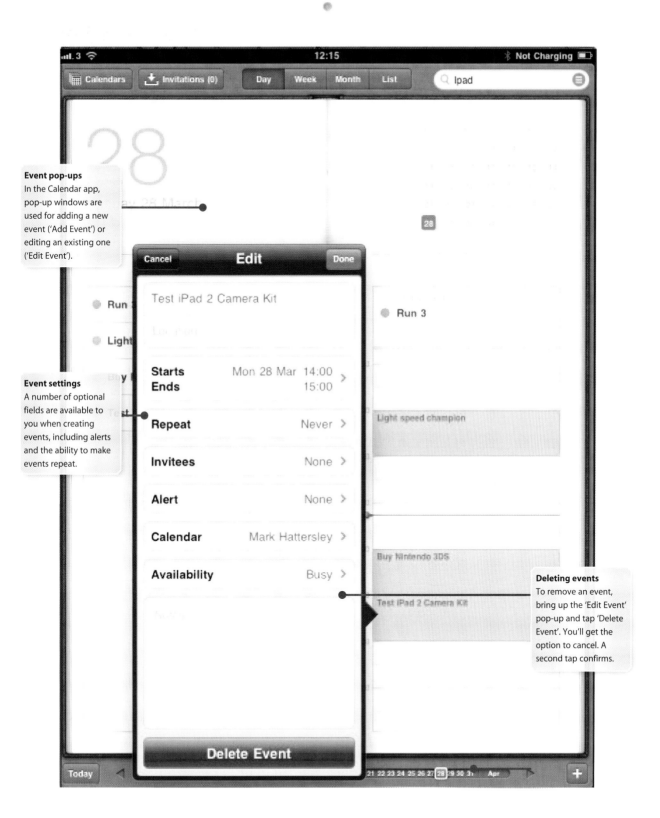

Event pop-ups
In the Calendar app, pop-up windows are used for adding a new event ('Add Event') or editing an existing one ('Edit Event').

Event settings
A number of optional fields are available to you when creating events, including alerts and the ability to make events repeat.

Deleting events
To remove an event, bring up the 'Edit Event' pop-up and tap 'Delete Event'. You'll get the option to cancel. A second tap confirms.

STEP BY STEP GUIDE: **Managing your calendar**

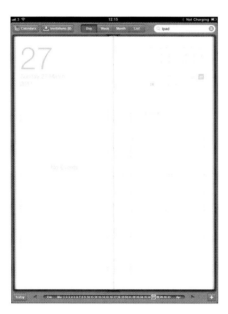

1 Check for clashes Before adding an appointment, check whether you've already got something to do at the same time. See the previous tutorial for steps to access the date in question.

2 Add an event Tap the '+' button at the bottom-right of the screen to bring up the 'Add Event' pop-up. If you decide at any time not to add the event, just tap 'Cancel'.

3 Add details Tap inside the 'Title' and 'Location' fields to add details of your event. Note that these elements will be searchable, so it pays to type in something reasonably descriptive.

4 Define a duration Tap the 'Starts/Ends' field to bring up the 'Start & End' pop-up. Select 'Starts' and use the spinner to define a time, and do the same for 'Ends'. Tap 'Done' when satisfied.

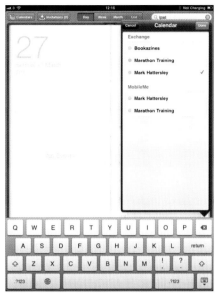

5 Set an alert Tap 'Alert' to set an event alert time. This appears as a notification at the set time. After setting an alert, you get the option to add a second one as well.

6 Pick a calendar If the event you're adding isn't meant to be part of your default calendar, tap 'Calendar' and select a different one. Take care here – this setting cannot be edited later.

Automate

There's not a great deal of point in manually adding a recurring event to your calendar over and over again: that's because the Calendar app lets you automate the process by way of its 'Repeat' menu item. Tap this to bring up the 'Repeat Event' pop-up. Here you can define an event to repeat daily, weekly, fortnightly, monthly, or annually.

7 Add notes Should your event need some information not covered by the basic details you've already put in, use the 'Notes' section. Be mindful, however, that notes are not searchable.

8 Edit events Most event details are editable. In day and list views, tap a selected event to see the 'Edit Event' pop-up. In week and month views, tap a selected event and then the 'Edit' button.

Using the address book to view and edit contacts

How to search, view and edit contacts on your iPad

LIKE ITS iPHONE EQUIVALENT, CONTACTS FOR iPAD is a pretty simple application, relying largely on data you send it via an iTunes sync. Contacts can also be synchronised with a variety of services (including Google Contacts and Yahoo! Address Book), along with information from Address Book for Mac OS X and Outlook 2003 or 2007 for Windows.

If you have set up groups of contacts using those applications or services, note that while you can view these groups using Contacts on the iPad, the app does not allow you to edit them.

When it comes to individual contact details, the iPad app is, thankfully, less restrictive. It's possible to add new contacts (which can, of course, later be sent back to your computer the next time you do a sync), and you can edit details for existing contacts, updating data and creating new fields as you like.

It's also possible to amend the sort order of your contacts. If you prefer the list order to be based on first names rather than surnames, select 'Mail, Contacts, Calendars' in the Settings app and set 'Sort Order' to 'First, Last'. Note that you can also amend a second option, 'Display Order', to 'Last, First'. This makes names in the app (both in the contacts list and individual contact pages) display like 'Jobs Steve' rather than 'Steve Jobs'. Neither of these options is permanent; if you want to go back to the default setting, simply go to the Settings app and reselect it.

KIT LIST:

- iPad
- Details of contacts (photos optional)

Time required: 10 mins
Difficulty: Beginner

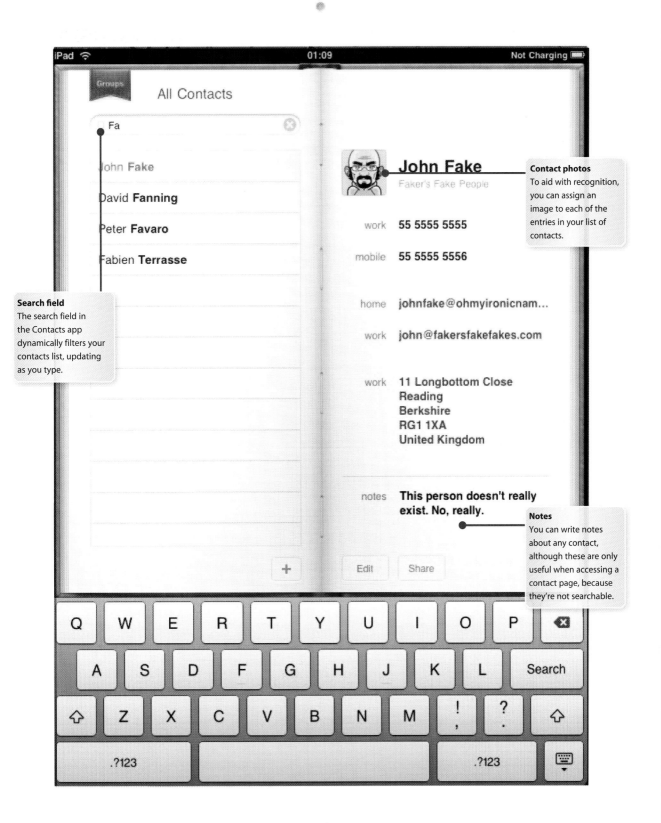

Groups   All Contacts

Fa ⊗

John **Fake**

David **Fanning**

Peter **Favaro**

Fabien **Terrasse**

John Fake
Faker's Fake People

work	**55 5555 5555**
mobile	**55 5555 5556**
home	johnfake@ohmyironicnam…
work	john@fakersfakefakes.com
work	**11 Longbottom Close** **Reading** **Berkshire** **RG1 1XA** **United Kingdom**
notes	**This person doesn't really** **exist. No, really.**

+   Edit   Share

Contact photos
To aid with recognition, you can assign an image to each of the entries in your list of contacts.

Search field
The search field in the Contacts app dynamically filters your contacts list, updating as you type.

Notes
You can write notes about any contact, although these are only useful when accessing a contact page, because they're not searchable.

Keyboard:
Q W E R T Y U I O P ⌫
A S D F G H J K L Search
⇧ Z X C V B N M ! , ? . ⇧
.?123   .?123 ⌨

STEP BY STEP GUIDE: Managing a contacts list

1 Find a contact Open a contact's page by selecting it from the list. Tap the letters on the left to snap to names matching the letter, or drag/flick to scroll the list manually.

2 See details A contact's details appear in the right-hand 'page' of the app. If the details are too long to be displayed, a scroll bar will briefly appear to signify this.

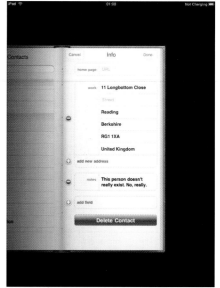

3 Edit details Tap the 'Edit' button at the foot of the page to amend information. Remove fields by tapping the red buttons, then tapping 'Delete'.

4 Removing a contact Scroll the page to the bottom and tap 'Delete Contact'. In the pop-up dialog, tap 'Delete' to confirm, otherwise 'Cancel'.

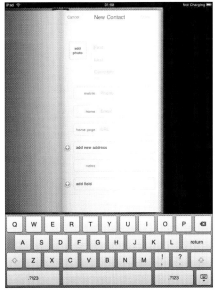

5 Forward a contact Tapping the 'Share' button brings up the standard email window so you can forward someone's details (as a VCF file).

6 Add a new contact To start, tap the '+' button at the bottom of the contacts list. A 'New Contact' page will appear.

More fields

To add specific details for a contact when in edit mode, scroll down and tap 'Add Field'. This brings up the 'Add Field' pop-up, enabling you to select a new field such as 'Birthday' or 'Job Title'. It's also possible to amend a field's type by selecting it while editing – for example, tap a telephone field to change it from 'home' or 'work' to 'Skype', 'iChat' or some other option.

7 Add a photo Tap 'add photo' and select an image from the 'Photo Albums' pop-up. Drag and pinch to move and scale the picture and tap 'Use' to add it to your contact's page.

8 Edit photos In edit mode, tap the photo for editing options: you can leave the photo as is ('Choose Existing Photo'), remove it ('Delete Photo'), or edit it ('Edit Photo', which offers 'Move and Scale' options).

Immerse yourself in online video with the YouTube app

Use your iPad to visit the world's most popular video site

SAYING THAT YOUTUBE IS POPULAR IS A BIT LIKE suggesting British people like a good moan about the weather – so obvious that it really doesn't bear repeating. But we'll repeat it anyway: YouTube is a popular website – really popular. From humble beginnings in 2005, the site grew extremely rapidly as broadband connections got faster and video-capable devices cheaper, with even relatively simple mobile phones able to capture video.

Today, YouTube is a behemoth. Its owners, Google, say that over 24 hours of video is uploaded every minute of the day. To put that in perspective, if you were to sit and watch everything that was uploaded to YouTube over the past 24 hours, you wouldn't be done for about four years – and that's if you didn't take breaks for things like eating and sleeping.

With such a huge amount of content ripe for discovery, you need an app that can help you find what you'd like to watch, and to share great videos with your friends. Luckily, the iPad's YouTube app is well designed, efficient and usable, making it easy to search YouTube, play videos and then build lists of favourites. The only slight niggle we noticed is that this version doesn't seem to enable you to create a YouTube account. While you don't need an account for storing favourites, we recommend you create one in Safari, because your favourites and subscriptions are then shared with YouTube wherever and however you access it.

KIT LIST:

■ **iPad**
■ **Internet connection**
■ **A YouTube account (for some features)**

Time required: 10 mins
Difficulty: Beginner

Want gaming tips?
If the fab Angry Birds iPad game is driving you crazy, you can actually find helpful walkthrough videos via the YouTube app.

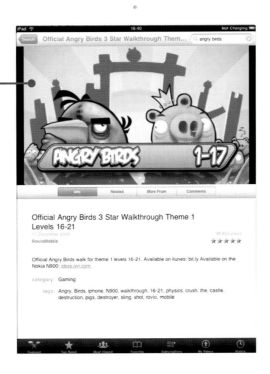

Control playback
Easy-to-use playback buttons, including a full-screen toggle, appear below the video.

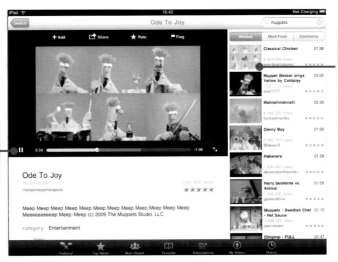

Landscape plus
With the iPad in landscape mode, YouTube shows your video full-screen. But tap the video and the 'Done' button and you get this nifty layout.

STEP BY STEP GUIDE: **Using the YouTube app**

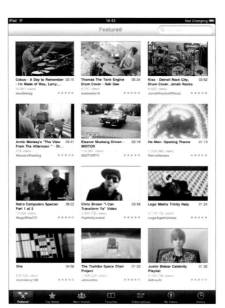

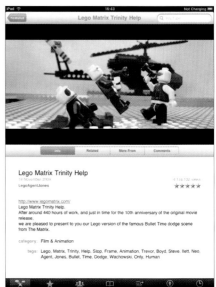

1 Find great videos On launching YouTube, use the search field to find videos you'd like to watch. Alternatively, use the 'Featured', 'Top Rated' and 'Most Viewed' toolbar buttons.

2 Play a video Tap a video to view it. It will load and start playing automatically. In portrait mode, the video's info will be displayed underneath. In landscape, video plays full-screen.

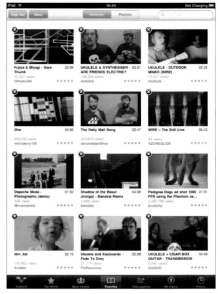

3 Sign in If you have a YouTube account, select 'Favorites' from the toolbar and click the 'Sign In' button at the top left. In the pop-up dialog, type your username and password and tap 'Sign In'.

4 View your favourites On signing in, any videos you've previously marked as favourites will be displayed. Tap 'Edit' to delete some favourites, and 'Done' once you've finished tidying.

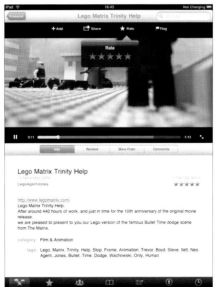

5 Add new favourites Adding a video to your 'Favorites' page is simple – tap the video and select 'Add' from the toolbar. In the 'Add Favorite' pop-up, select 'Favorites' (or, if signed in, a playlist).

6 Share and rate videos The toolbar can also be used to share and rate videos. Tap 'Share' and Mail opens, enabling you to send a link to that video. To rate, tap 'Rate' and one of the stars.

Lost favourite

Have you recently seen a great YouTube video on your iPad but forgotten the details? Visited your 'Favorites' page and realised, with a sinking feeling, that you forgot to set the video as a favourite? Don't fret, because the YouTube app is there for you with its cunning 'History' toolbar button. Tap it and you get a list of all the videos you've recently watched.

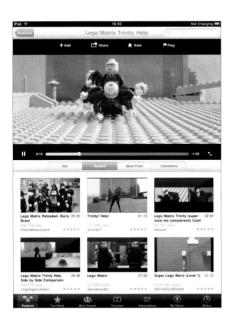

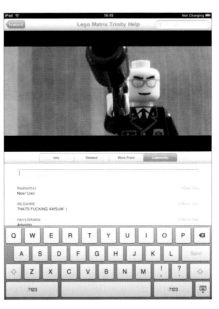

7 Find related videos If you like a particular video, use the 'Related' tab to find similar videos. Alternatively, tap 'More From' to see content from whoever uploaded that video.

8 Interact Use the 'Comments' tab to see what other people have said about the current video. Tap 'Add a comment' and the keyboard appears for you to type some thoughts and tap 'Send'.

Viewing photos and creating your own slideshows

Learn about the Photos app and the iPad's Picture Frame feature

AS SOON AS YOU SEE THE GORGEOUS iPAD DISPLAY,
you know that it's going to be just perfect for photos.
The photographs you sync with your desktop or laptop
computer (along with screen grabs taken by pressing the
Home and Sleep buttons together, and images saved to
your iPad by apps) are all made available in Photos.

Photos is another example of an iPad app that's more or less a direct
translation of its iPhone sibling, but on the iPad the experience has been
boosted by an order of magnitude, thanks to the larger screen and a few
additional touches. Perhaps the most interesting thing about the iPad Photos
app is how fun and tactile it feels. By contrast, the iPhone's Photos app, with its
rigid scrolling, feels quite sterile.

Although the iPhone app's gestures – tap to open, back buttons to close/go
up one level in the hierarchy – work with the iPad Photos app, you can also
rapidly spread two fingers over an album or image to open it, or quickly pinch
to close something. When you have a photo displayed full-screen and tap it, a
scrubbing bar appears, making it easy to rapidly navigate huge albums and find
the photo you want.

In addition to these features, both the Photos app and the iPad's lock screen
enable you to create configurable slideshows. This means that your iPad not only
makes a great digital photo album, but is also, during 'downtime', a first-rate
digital photo frame.

KIT LIST:

■ **iPad with some
pictures stored**

Time required: 10 mins
Difficulty: Beginner

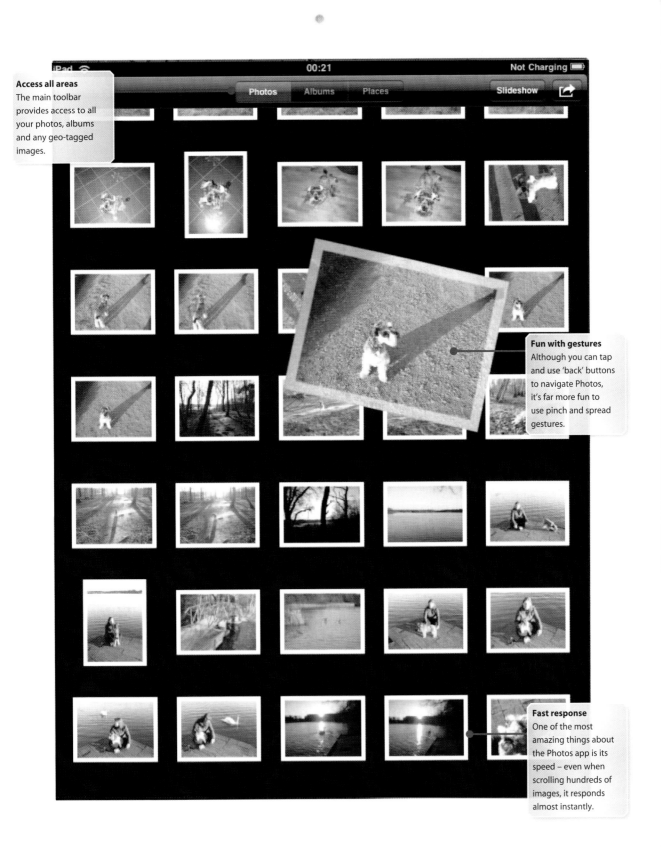

Access all areas
The main toolbar provides access to all your photos, albums and any geo-tagged images.

Fun with gestures
Although you can tap and use 'back' buttons to navigate Photos, it's far more fun to use pinch and spread gestures.

Fast response
One of the most amazing things about the Photos app is its speed – even when scrolling hundreds of images, it responds almost instantly.

STEP BY STEP GUIDE: **Using the Photos app**

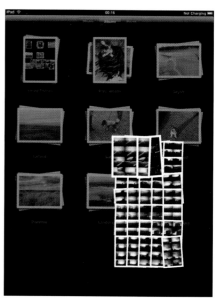

1 View photo albums Albums kept in sync via iTunes are shown by default, or when you click the 'Albums' button. 'Saved Photos' houses screen grabs taken on the iPad and images saved by apps.

2 Peek within Each album is represented by a pile of photos, which you can peek inside using a 'spread' gesture. Move your fingers from the screen and the pile returns to its starting point.

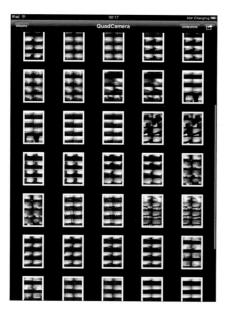

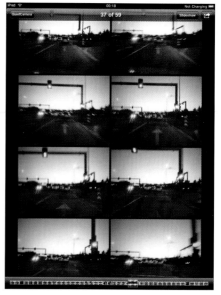

3 Explore an album Tap a pile (or do a kind of 'flick spread') and the entire album is displayed. If there are too many thumbnails for the screen, you can drag- or flick-scroll vertically.

4 View images Tap an image for a full-screen view. Tap again to see controls and info. Swipe to see the next or previous image. For faster navigation, use the scrub bar at the bottom.

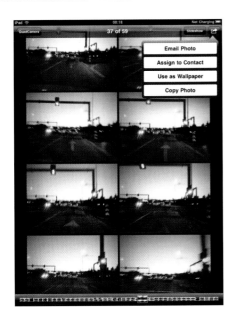

5 Use actions Perform actions on the current image (email, assign to a contact, use as wallpaper, copy) by tapping the button at the top right of the screen and making a selection.

6 Create a slideshow Tap the 'Slideshow' button for slideshow options. Define whether you want music and what kind of transition you'd like between images, and then tap 'Start Slideshow'.

Slideshows

If you like slideshows, take a trip to the Settings app. In the 'Photos' section, you can define how long each image is displayed in Photos app slideshows, along with whether slideshows repeat or shuffle. Select 'Picture Frame' to define options for slideshows activated by the picture-frame button on the iPad's lock screen. Tap 'Albums' to select albums for inclusion; alternatively, 'All Photos' makes the slideshow use all of your images.

7 View all photos Back at the albums screen (tap the top-left button or pinch a couple of times to get to it), tap the 'Photos' button for a view that shows all of the photos on your iPad.

8 Examine places If you have geo-tagged photos, tap the 'Places' button. You'll see pins where photos have been taken. Tap a pin to see a pile of photos from that location.

Subscribe to Macworld

Save a bundle and get each issue delivered to your door

Macworld regulars can get every issue delivered straight to their door, and save 83 per cent from the cover price by taking out a subscription direct with us.

If you subscribe to Macworld we can cut out the middlemen, and then pass the saving (over £15) straight back to you.

With a Macworld subscription, you'll get the magazine delivered right to your door, so you don't have to keep an eye out for copies of Macworld at the newsagents. We also deliver the first run from the press direct to our subscribers, so they're always the first to get the latest information. And it's a great way to support your favourite magazine.

Macworld is created by an international team of experts based in London and San Francisco who live, eat and dream Apple

Get all this

✓ Every issue delivered directly to your door

✓ Save 83 per cent off of the cover price

✓ Be the first to read each issue with priority delivery

Read Macworld on an iPad & iPhone

Digital Magazines
You can read all your favourite magazines on your iPad, iPhone, or on your computer. At the Zinio UK store you'll find digital versions of magazines like iPad & iPhone User, Macworld, and books like this Complete Guide To the iPad 2. Each title contains exactly the same material as appears in the print version. Get ready to join the digital revolution!
www.macworld.co.uk/zinio

App Store Apps
Macworld has an incredible iPhone app that enables you to read all its amazing content in a beautiful interface designed especially for the iPhone. The Macworld app is packed with topic-based feeds enabling you to focus on articles that interest you. Topics such as iPad, iPhone & iPod, Mac, Mac Software, Creative, Business, and Education.
www.macworld.co.uk/iphone

Call 01858 438 867 and quote CGi2

• Be the first to read Macworld

and save 83%

Message from the editor

The very first issue of Macworld was published back in 1984, just as Apple launched the first Mac. Since then Macworld has followed Apple religiously. We've been there at every Expo, every product launch, we've had our hands on every new piece of kit. We've been with Apple through the highs and the lows. We know Apple. Macworld is created by an international team of experts based in London and San Francisco, who live, eat and dream Apple.

Our contributors include specialists who use Macs at work: designers and illustrators, professional photographers, animators, musicians, developers and more.

If you are new to Apple and are looking for advice to help you get started, or if you are a Mac fanatic looking to justify your next buy, Macworld is the magazine to ensure you make the right decision. And then we'll help you get the most out of the world's best computer, to be more productive and creative than you ever thought possible.

Join the Macworld team every issue as we analyse the latest product announcements from the world's biggest (and still the best) technology company.

Karen Haslam,
editor@macworld.co.uk

Macworld Social

We're a pretty social bunch here at Macworld, and we're happy to chat to readers. You can email us on team@ macworld.co.uk or use any of these social networks...

www.facebook.com/macworlduk

www.twitter.com/macworlduk

http://lnkd.in/GQgUU7

www.macworld.co.uk/forum

TERMS & CONDITIONS

- No obligation – we'll give you a full refund on any unmailed issues if you ever decide to cancel
- After three issues for £3 Macworld subscription will continue at the discounted rate of £40.00 for 14 issues
- For subscribers paying by cheque or credit card, subscription rate is £54.99 for 12 months
- You'll receive 14 issues in a 12-month subscription
- Your subscription will start with the next available issue
- For overseas rates please call +44 1858 438 867 and quote reference CGi2

Creating and working with text documents in Pages

Learn how to edit and format text with Apple's iPad word processor

WHEN STEVE JOBS DEMOED THE iPAD, THE iWORK apps wowed more than anything else. Here was proof that the iPad wasn't only about consuming content; it was about creating it, too, and with Apple-developed apps no less. In reality, though, Pages for iPad – which you can buy from the App Store, either by itself or as part of iWork – isn't the same application as Pages for the Mac. In use, it feels rather like Pages 'lite'.

However, despite missing a number of features many writers take for granted (such as a live word count), Pages for iPad is an interesting and important piece of software. Apple designed many aspects of the app from the ground up, ensuring that it is suitable for the touch-based iPad interface rather than being a clunky port of the desktop application.

Once you've used Pages for a while, the way it works will become second nature, but it might take a while to get over the absence of certain features familiar from desktop applications. For example, there's no 'Save' command – Pages just saves your work as you create it. Therefore, if you need to retain a particular version of a document, you must duplicate it before continuing.

Also, the application lacks most of the toolbars and palettes featured in desktop word processors. In fact, in landscape view, Pages is a full-screen app that shows only your work and the virtual keyboard. Instead, tools are presented in context, as you need them.

KIT LIST:

■ **iPad**
■ **Pages for iPad**

Time required: 10 mins
Difficulty: Beginner

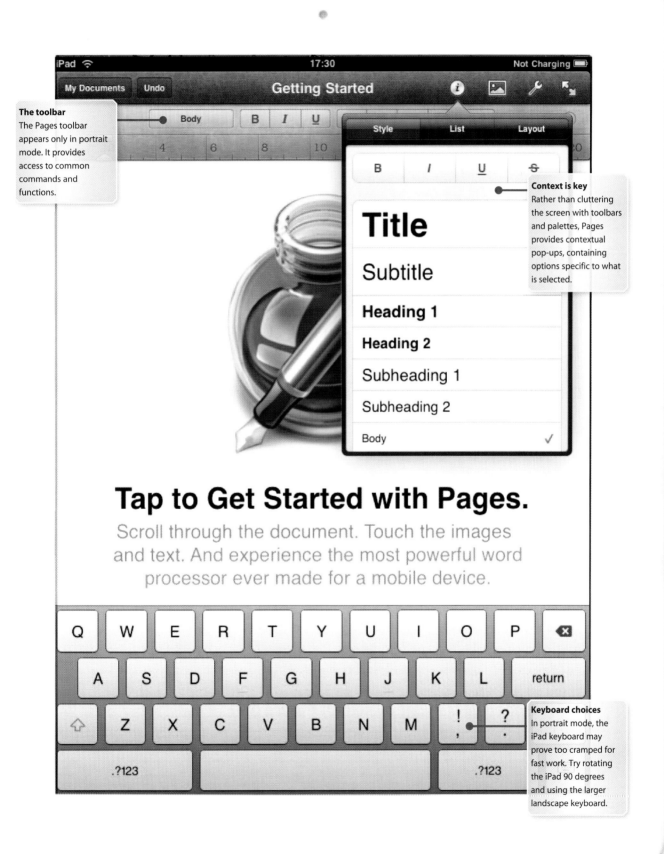

The toolbar
The Pages toolbar appears only in portrait mode. It provides access to common commands and functions.

iPad
17:30
Not Charging

My Documents | Undo | Getting Started

Body | B | I | U

Style | List | Layout

B | I | U | S̶

Context is key
Rather than cluttering the screen with toolbars and palettes, Pages provides contextual pop-ups, containing options specific to what is selected.

Title

Subtitle

Heading 1

Heading 2

Subheading 1

Subheading 2

Body ✓

Tap to Get Started with Pages.

Scroll through the document. Touch the images and text. And experience the most powerful word processor ever made for a mobile device.

Keyboard choices
In portrait mode, the iPad keyboard may prove too cramped for fast work. Try rotating the iPad 90 degrees and using the larger landscape keyboard.

STEP BY STEP GUIDE: Working in Pages for iPad

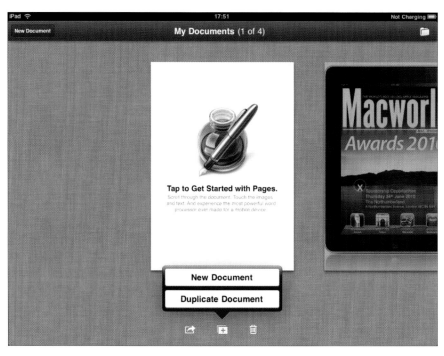

1 See all your Pages documents Saved Pages documents are shown when you launch the app – swipe to view more. The sharing button at the bottom left provides email, share and export options.

2 Delete or duplicate To get rid of a document, tap the trash icon and tap 'Delete Document' (there's no undo for this). The central button lets you duplicate a document.

3 Create a new document Tap 'New Document' to access 15 Pages templates and a blank document. Tap any template to work in it.

4 Edit content Default content and styles already exist in templates. Delete components you don't want or type in elements to add your content.

5 Go full-screen With your iPad in landscape orientation, Pages moves into full-screen mode, removing the 'distraction' of the toolbar, and enlarging the text and keyboard to make typing easier.

6 Check spelling If you mis-spell a word, Pages usually auto-corrects it. If it doesn't, you'll see a squiggly red underline. Tap the word for possible replacements and tap to select one.

Look it up

Pages includes a built-in dictionary. If you're unsure of the meaning of a word you've put in your document, double-tap the word to make a selection, tap 'More...', and then tap 'Definition...'. If a definition for the selected word is available, it will be displayed in a scrollable pop-up window. Tap outside the pop-up to close it.

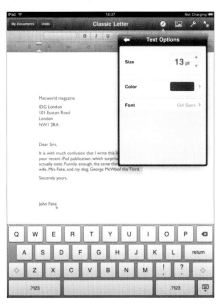

7 Undo and redo To erase your last change, tap the toolbar's 'Undo' button. You can redo it by tap-holding 'Undo' to get the pop-up menu shown.

8 Change the font Select some text, tap the 'Info' button, select 'Text Options' and make the desired changes.

Formatting text and using images in Pages

Learn about text-wrapping, columns, styles and more

WORD PROCESSING HAS COME A LONG WAY IN a short space of time. Early word processors were little more than digital typewriters, but in recent years they've increasingly borrowed from desktop-publishing software. Creating documents is more than choosing a font – users demand the ability to work with images, structure a document both semantically and visually, and create something that looks great.

Pages for iPad includes a number of features that enable you to give your work some professional-looking visual punch. First and foremost, built-in styles enable you to use titles, headings, bullets and captions to structure your document and keep text looking consistent throughout. For those occasions where something needs to stand out, you can override colours and fonts.

Images, too, are a big part of Pages. You can drop images stored in the Photos app into Pages documents, and once you've inserted an image, it can be resized, scaled within its boundaries via a double-tap and slider combo, and rotated by a tap-hold and use of a second finger. Importantly, you can also define how text and images interact, adjusting text-wrapping in several different ways.

The walkthrough covers all these things, along with creating columns of text. Our example is pretty basic from a layout standpoint, but that's intentional – we're providing you with the building blocks. Once you've mastered them you should be able to create increasingly elaborate documents. Also, remember to experiment with Pages templates for layout ideas and extra styles.

KIT LIST:

■ iPad
■ Pages for iPad

Time required: 10 mins
Difficulty: Beginner

iPad 20:25 Not Charging

Part 5: Sharing Your Work on the Web

iWork.com makes it easy to send your document.

Share with others, or just yourself

Tap the My Documents button in the toolbar to view all your documents. Select "Share via iWork.com" from the menu. Sign in, invite friends or co-workers, the to upload to the web.

With iWork.com, anyone on a Mac or and post comments, or download a ver or PD format.

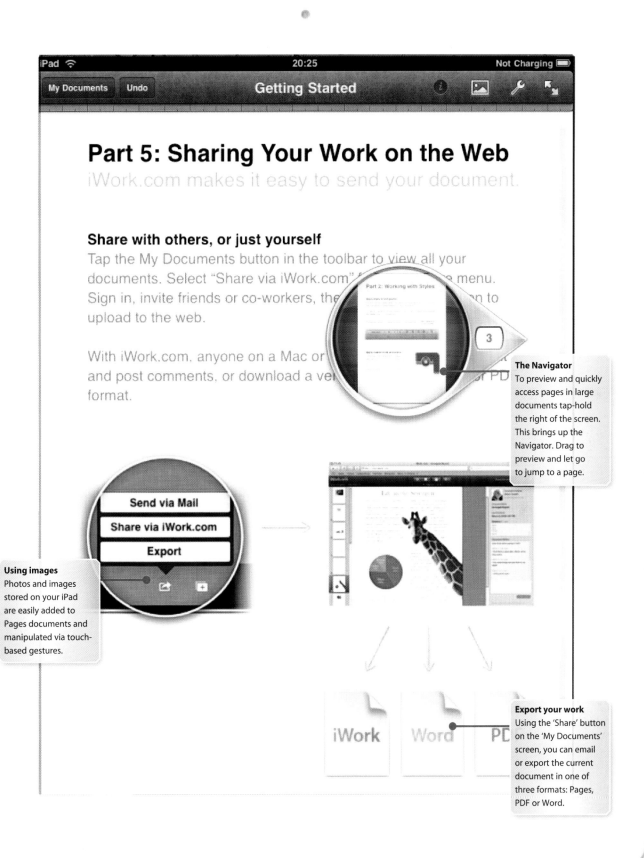

The Navigator
To preview and quickly access pages in large documents tap-hold the right of the screen. This brings up the Navigator. Drag to preview and let go to jump to a page.

Send via Mail

Share via iWork.com

Export

Using images
Photos and images stored on your iPad are easily added to Pages documents and manipulated via touch-based gestures.

iWork   Word   PD

Export your work
Using the 'Share' button on the 'My Documents' screen, you can email or export the current document in one of three formats: Pages, PDF or Word.

STEP BY STEP GUIDE: **Exploring Pages in more depth**

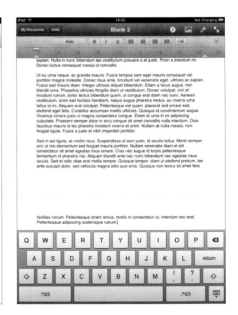

1 Grab some text If you don't have any text to use in your document, open Safari, head to lipsum.com and create and copy a few paragraphs of placeholder text.

2 Create a new document In Pages, create a new document using the Blank template. Tap anywhere on the page and select 'Paste' from the pop-up to paste your text.

3 Add an image Tap the Insert menu and select an image from the 'Media' tab. It will be added to your document, roughly wherever the insert pointer was positioned.

4 Resize the image Tap the image and drag the bottom-left drag handle right and up. As the image reduces in size, its dimensions are shown and text automatically reflows around it.

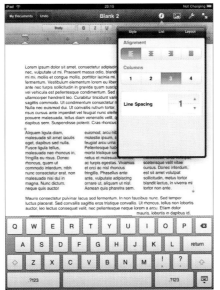

5 Turn off text-wrapping To stop text wrapping around an image, select the image, tap the Info menu, select the 'Arrange' tab and choose 'Above and Below' from the 'Wrap' sub-menu.

6 Try columns If you'd like to reformat text into columns, select it and then tap the Info menu. In the 'Layout' tab, select the number of columns you'd like and Pages reflows your text.

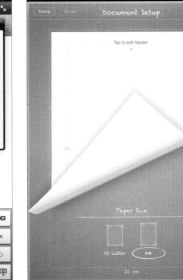

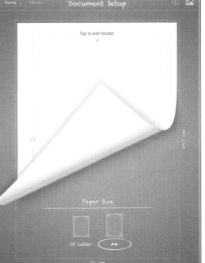

7 Utilise styles Although you can change the appearance of text via the 'Style' tab of the Info menu, use predefined styles for a title, headings and captions to keep your work consistent.

8 Edit document settings Select 'Document Setup' from the Tools menu to amend global settings, including the header and footer size, document margins and paper size.

Looking good
Because Apple is interested in how your work comes across visually, rather than just the content, the iWork apps share various capabilities, including an ability to create tables. Of course, some apps are more suited to certain tasks. Note therefore that to put a chart into a Pages document, it may be easiest to work in Numbers. Start with a form and use this to populate a table that can be turned into a chart. You can then copy the chart in Numbers and paste it into your Pages document.

Setting up spreadsheets in Apple's Numbers

Learn about how to create tables and forms

IF WE TAKE A TERRIFYING TRIP TO THE DISTANT past (well, 1979), we'd find it was Apple that popularised the spreadsheet. The first example of its type, Dan Bricklin and Bob Frankston's VisiCalc, was first available for the Apple II, and it catapulted the Apple II from being a hobbyist computer to an important tool in business.

In the modern age, Microsoft Excel is the spreadsheet everyone knows, and so it's perhaps fitting that its biggest challenger on the Mac – and the first app in years to really try something new with spreadsheets – is Numbers, part of Apple's iWork suite.

Numbers for iPad retains many of its Mac cousin's best features: it's powerful and easy to use, and it's flexible in terms of layout. Rather than restricting individual sheets to a table with the odd embedded chart, Numbers enables you to place multiple tables within a sheet and add whatever text and images you want.

There's an awful lot to explore with spreadsheet applications, and so for the walkthrough we've decided to lead you through the process of creating a basic table for a list of apps with release dates, prices and ratings. This will enable you to get to grips with resizing a basic table, defining data types for columns and building a form for faster data input.

In the tutorial after this one, we'll show you how to take a similar table and output calculations and graphs.

KIT LIST:

- iPad
- Numbers for iPad

Time required: 15 mins
Difficulty: Intermediate

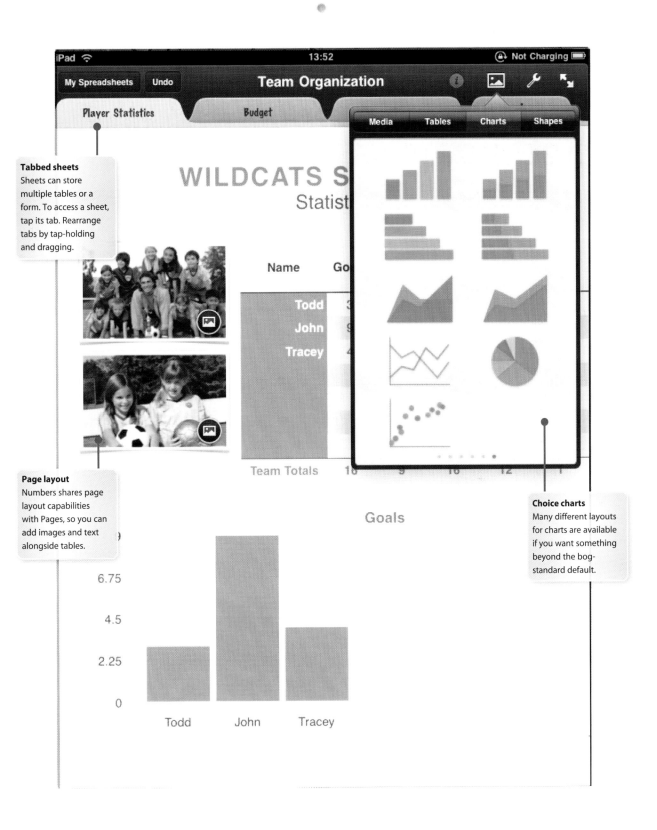

Tabbed sheets
Sheets can store multiple tables or a form. To access a sheet, tap its tab. Rearrange tabs by tap-holding and dragging.

Page layout
Numbers shares page layout capabilities with Pages, so you can add images and text alongside tables.

Choice charts
Many different layouts for charts are available if you want something beyond the bog-standard default.

STEP BY STEP GUIDE: Getting started with Numbers

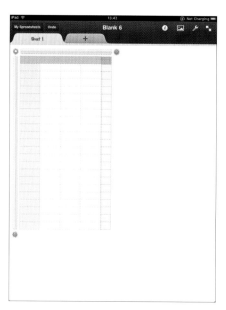

1 New table Tap 'New Spreadsheet' and select 'Blank'. Tap the table to select it and tap its table handle (the top-left 'button'). Drag the column handle leftwards until there are only four columns.

2 Fine-tune the table Use the bottom-right drag handle to stretch the table to the width of the page. In the Info menu, tap 'Table Options' and 'Alternating Rows' to make the table striped.

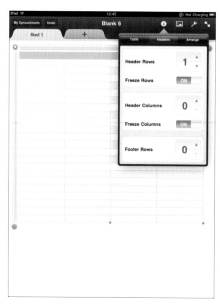

3 Define headers Tap the 'Headers' tab in the Info menu and set 'Header Columns' to zero. The latter step means the leftmost column contains table entries rather than headers.

4 Add your header Double-tap the first header to bring up the keyboard. Type 'App name'. Tap the next header and type 'Price'. Type 'Release date' and 'Rating' in the final two headers.

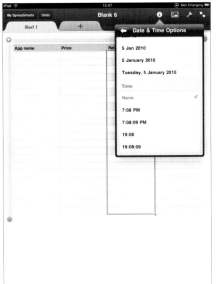

5 Set column types Double-tap the column bar above 'App name' to select the column. Select 'Format' from the Info menu and double-tap 'Text'. Similarly, format the second column as 'Currency'.

6 Finish column types Select the third column and set the format to 'Date & Time'. From the sub-menu, select a date option and 'None' from 'Time'. Set the final column's format to 'Star Rating'.

Top table
After you've completed your table, you can change the way it looks. Tap the table and select it using the table handle. In the Info menu, select the 'Table' tab and choose one of the layout options. Use 'Table Options' to further refine your table's visual appearance, including an optional table name row, alternating rows (table stripes), table borders and grid options.

7 Create a form Tap the '+' tab and select 'New Form'. Choose 'Table 1' (meaning the table you created) and you get form-based input for your table, with pre-defined field types.

8 Need to reorganise the table?
Select the table and single-tap the column- or row-bar to select a column or row. Tap-hold and drag it to its new position.

Calculating with Numbers and plotting the results

Use basic formulae to work with data and then chart the results

IN THE PREVIOUS TUTORIAL, WE WORKED THROUGH the basics of creating a table and filling it with content. Of course, much of the point of spreadsheets is not in merely displaying information but in manipulating and processing data. In the walkthrough here we look at two features of Numbers that do just that.

KIT LIST:

■ **iPad**
■ **Numbers for iPad**

Time required: 15 mins
Difficulty: Intermediate

The first feature is the use of a formula – in our example, to calculate an average from a column of numbers. Of course this is one of the most basic formulae you can use in a spreadsheet, but what we're interested in is how the process works in Numbers.

The second feature is the ability to link a chart to a table. With charts that are dynamically updated, Numbers makes displaying data in a visually appealing way both easy and quick, and it's worth noting that you can potentially save yourself even more time. When you create a new spreadsheet, take a good look at the 15 templates supplied as they can be readily adapted to your needs. Examples Apple has provided for you to experiment with include a combined weight-loss and running log, documents related to office administration (invoices, expenses, employee schedules) and a mortgage calculator.

While working on the walkthrough, we noticed that fields would occasionally 'forget' values and semi-randomly revert to being blank. Hitting the 'Home' button, relaunching Numbers and opening the spreadsheet again seemed to deal with this.

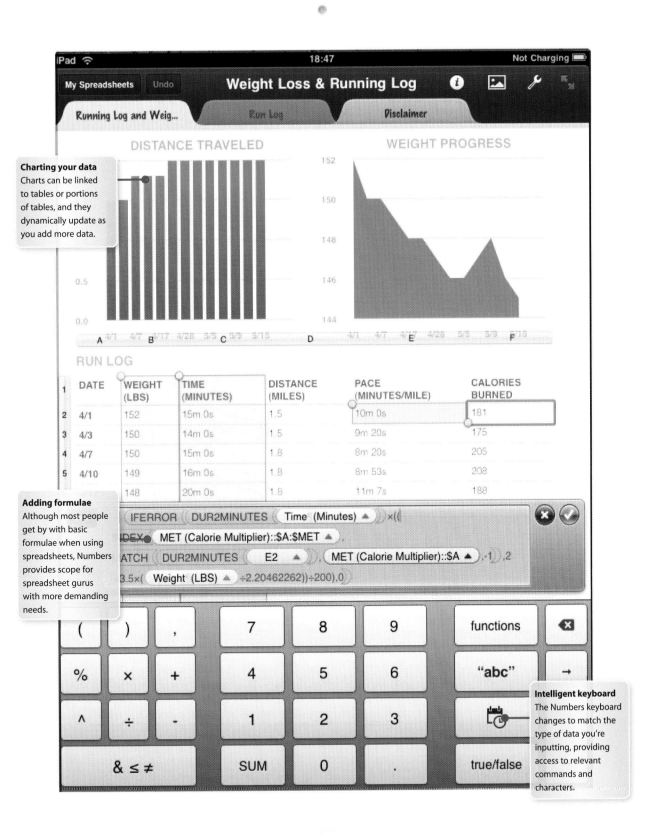

Charting your data
Charts can be linked to tables or portions of tables, and they dynamically update as you add more data.

Adding formulae
Although most people get by with basic formulae when using spreadsheets, Numbers provides scope for spreadsheet gurus with more demanding needs.

Intelligent keyboard
The Numbers keyboard changes to match the type of data you're inputting, providing access to relevant commands and characters.

STEP BY STEP GUIDE: **Exploring Numbers in more depth**

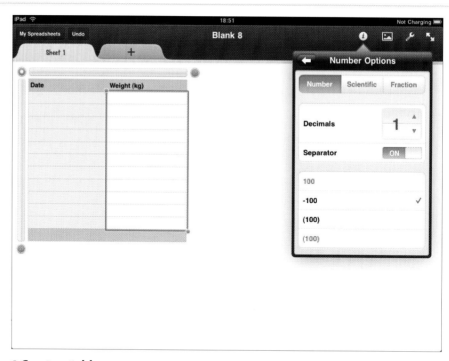

1 Create a table Set up a two-column table akin to the one in the previous tutorial, but ignore step 3 and leave header columns in place. In the 'Headers' tab of the Info menu, set 'Footer Rows' to 1.

2 Define the columns Set the format of the left-hand column to a date with no time (see step 6 of the previous tutorial) and the weight column to the number format with one decimal point.

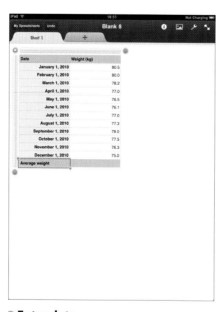

3 Enter data Input values into the columns as shown. Enter 'Average weight' on the bottom left and right-align it using the 'Cells' tab of the Info menu.

4 Add a formula Double-tap the bottom right cell and tap the '=' button. To find the average, tap 'SUM' and type '÷12'. Tap the tick mark to finish.

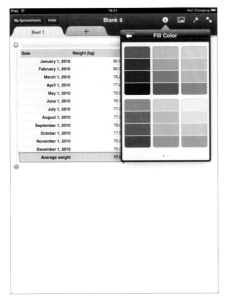

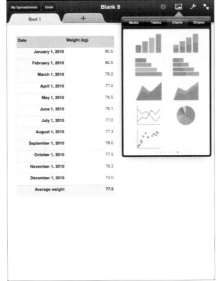

5 Make the footer stand out Tap the left cell, drag the selection to cover both cells, select 'Cells', tap 'Fill Color' and select a colour.

6 Add a chart From the Insert button, select the 'Charts' tab and the type of chart to link to your table. You can swipe to see additional choices.

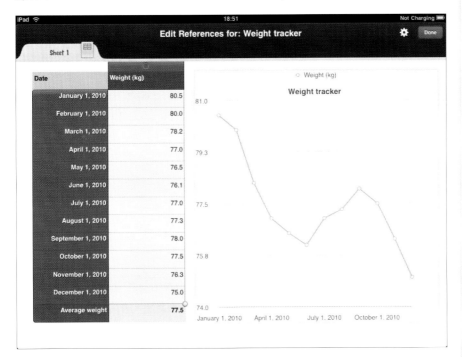

7 Link the chart Double-tap the chart, then tap the weight column's header. Numbers should automatically plot all of the values. If not, move the drag handle at the bottom right.

8 Improve the layout With layouts that involve a table and chart, it's often better to use your iPad in landscape view and resize the page components so they take up more of the screen.

Quick change
If you need to to change some specific values in your tables, it's good to make use of the find-and-replace functionality within Numbers (and, indeed, throughout the iWorks suite). Select 'Find' from the Tools menu, and tap the cog icon to access the 'Find' options. Tap 'Find and Replace', type your terms into the two fields provided, and then tap 'Replace'.

Creating simple presentations in Keynote

Learn how to add slides, edit template content and more

APPLE'S LONG ASSOCIATION WITH DESKTOP
publishing was evident in the way iWork was devised.
Instead of apeing the fairly matter-of-fact style of
Microsoft Office, iWork mixed and matched Office-style
workflow and features with DTP-oriented layout and
ease of use that is classic Apple. The result was a suite
that helps you easily create documents that both say what they need to say
and look beautiful.

Keynote is Apple's answer to PowerPoint, and while the iPad version is
simplified somewhat from its desktop cousin, it nonetheless gives you
everything you need to make a high-quality presentation on the move.

The app gives you a helping hand throughout. A dozen built-in templates
provide a great starting point, and, sensibly, Apple has made three of them quite
plain, so they're suitable for almost any subject matter. When adding a new
slide, you get to choose from one of eight basic layouts (one of which is blank),
because on the iPad it's often quicker to replace placeholder content than to
start from scratch.

And like the other apps in the iWork stable, Keynote has a context-sensitive
workflow. This provides you with the tools you need to perform a task on the
item selected, rather than cluttering up the screen with toolbars and palettes.

Here we'll deal with the basics of Keynote – we've saved animations and other
attention-grabbing features for a subsequent tutorial.

KIT LIST:

■ **iPad**
■ **Keynote for iPad**

Time required: 10 mins
Difficulty: Intermediate

Keynote themes
The iPad version of Keynote has a dozen built-in themes, including three basic ones – the top row here – that just have a plain background.

Landscape-only
Unlike the other iWork apps, Keynote is always in landscape mode. Turn your iPad to portrait orientation… and nothing happens.

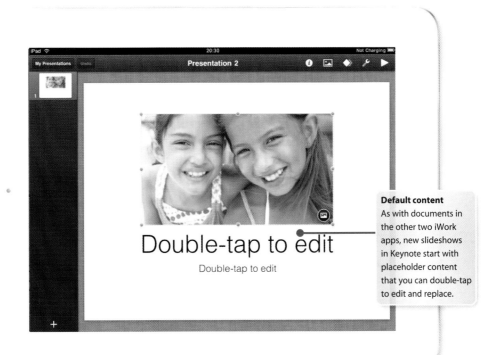

Default content
As with documents in the other two iWork apps, new slideshows in Keynote start with placeholder content that you can double-tap to edit and replace.

STEP BY STEP GUIDE: **Keynote basics**

1 Add and edit a new slide To add a new slide, tap the sidebar's '+' button and then tap your preferred layout. To edit existing content, double-tap it and make changes using the contextual tools.

2 Add an image Tap the Insert menu, select 'Media' and choose an image to add it to your presentation. The Insert menu also houses tables, charts and shapes for you to use.

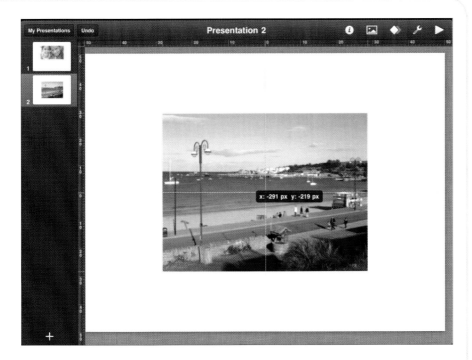

3 Edit the image Single-tap your image to resize it using the drag handles or reposition it via drag (rules and guides automatically appear). Double-tap to scale the image within its boundary.

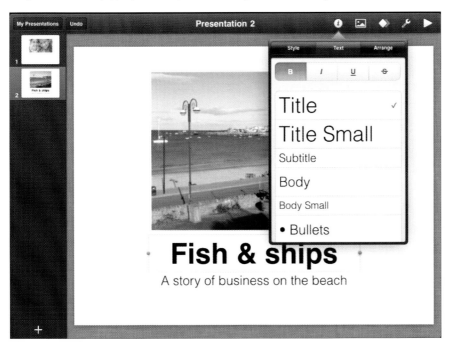

4 Add text Add a text box by tapping the 'T' in the 'Shapes' tab within the Insert menu. To format the text, select its box and then select options in the Info menu's 'Text' tab.

Moving slides

To change the order of your slides, tap-holding a slide in the sidebar until the slide starts pulsating, at which point you can drag it to a new location. If you want to move several slides, tap-hold one and then select more with another finger. The selection needn't be contiguous. You can then tap-hold to pick up the pile of slides and move the lot.

Creating eye-catching Keynote presentations

Take advantage of animations, image styles, Magic Move and more

THE REAL POWER OF KEYNOTE LIES IN ITS EASE
of use and its ability to produce presentations that look
far better than those created in rival applications. To that
end, this tutorial concentrates on boosting the visual
appeal of your presentations, by enhancing images,
arranging items, and working with transitions.

As in the other iWork apps, you can give images a distinctive look using the
'Style' tab in the Info menu. Initially, this gives you half a dozen styles that are
quite tasteful, emphasising images via subtle drop shadows and well-designed
borders. More options are available via the Style Options menu, although most
of the examples in the 'Border' tab are a bit over the top.

The Info menu also houses the 'Arrange' tab. This contains important controls
for flipping content and moving objects forward or back.

Once you start really getting into the visual side of your presentations, you
might hanker for precision placement, and Keynote enables this. Drag any item
and you'll see grids and pixel coordinates. If the item is aligned centrally, a yellow
guide will temporarily appear. You can also pinch to zoom out or spread your
fingers to zoom in.

If you zoom in so much that your slide is bigger than the workspace area, you'll
go into full-screen mode, at which point the sidebar and toolbar are accessed by
tapping relevant screen edges. For further precision, you can zoom any area of a
slide to 200 per cent.

KIT LIST:

■ **iPad**
■ **Keynote for iPad**

Time required: 15 mins
Difficulty: Intermediate

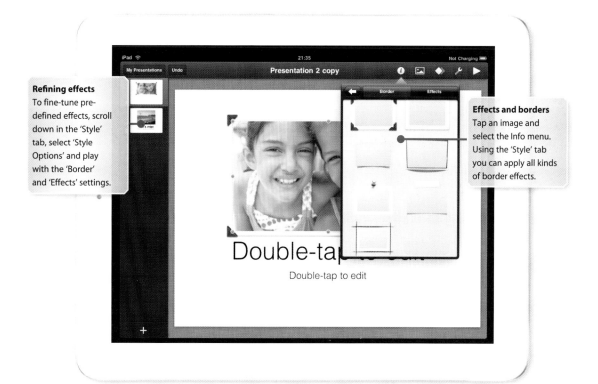

Refining effects
To fine-tune pre-defined effects, scroll down in the 'Style' tab, select 'Style Options' and play with the 'Border' and 'Effects' settings.

Effects and borders
Tap an image and select the Info menu. Using the 'Style' tab you can apply all kinds of border effects.

Slide management
Tap a slide in Keynote's sidebar to see a menu with which you can cut, copy, paste or delete a slide.

STEP BY STEP GUIDE: Jazzing up presentations

1 Work with duplicates To retain a previous slide's layout, tap it in the sidebar, select 'Copy', then select 'Paste'. To change the image, tap it, select 'Replace...' and choose a new image.

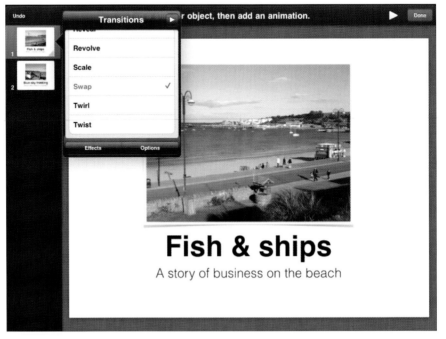

2 Add transitions To add an animated transition, tap a slide, tap the Animation menu, tap the menu that appears next to the slide and choose a transition to preview it. Tap 'Done' to confirm.

3 Advanced selection To apply settings to multiple items, select them all by tap-holding one and tapping others. When they're all selected, make your changes via the Info menu.

4 Preview your presentation You can preview your presentation at any point. Tap the 'Play' button to start your presentation; tap or swipe left for the next slide and swipe right for the previous one.

Magic Move

If you want to create complex animations between two slides, use Keynote's Magic Move feature. It automatically creates transitions between objects on adjacent slides that are identical. To start, select 'Magic Move...' from the 'Transitions' pop-up. If you already have a duplicate slide, tap 'No', otherwise tap 'Yes' to duplicate your slide. All you then need to do is make your changes to the second slide and Keynote does the rest.

Keep track of your data with Bento for iPad

How to use iPad Bento – the database tool for the rest of us

BENTO FOR THE iPHONE AND iPOD TOUCH WAS one of the first apps to really show what the iPhone OS could do in terms of running high-powered and fully featured apps – and now it's available on the iPad. It's a database tool from FileMaker – the company is behind the business database tool called (unimaginatively) FileMaker. Bento is the easier-to-use, easier-on-the-eye database program for consumers to keep track of anything from credit cards to sports teams. It offers 25 ready-to-use and editable templates, including handy tools for event planning, to do lists, recipes and small business and client management.

Bento syncs wirelessly with Bento 4 for Mac. While this expands what Bento can do, the standalone iPad app remains powerful enough to help you keep things together without using your desktop computer at all. Used with a Mac, Bento will sync your databases, so that the copies on your Mac and on your iPad are bang up to date. This is done over a WiFi connection, and your iPad and Mac need to be on the same network.

Bento 4 costs £29.99 for a single licence, or £59.99 for a family pack, which entitles you to install the software on up to five computers. Bento for iPad is a steal at £2.99 – if you just want it for your iPad you'll save a packet.

In this example, we describe creating a home inventory (perfect for landlords and tenants!), but you can use the same basic technique to keep an eye on books you lend to others, for example.

KIT LIST:

- iPad
- Bento app, £2.99 from iTunes App Store
- Bento app on your Mac optional; £29.99

Time required: 10 mins
Difficulty: Beginner

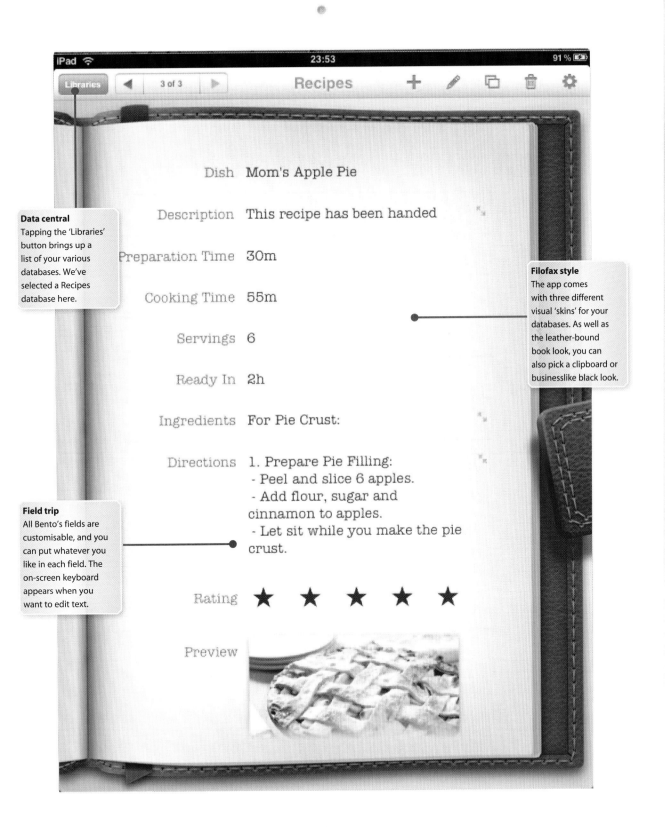

Dish   Mom's Apple Pie

Description   This recipe has been handed

Preparation Time   30m

Cooking Time   55m

Servings   6

Ready In   2h

Ingredients   For Pie Crust:

Directions   1. Prepare Pie Filling:
- Peel and slice 6 apples.
- Add flour, sugar and
cinnamon to apples.
- Let sit while you make the pie
crust.

Rating   ★ ★ ★ ★ ★

Preview

Data central
Tapping the 'Libraries' button brings up a list of your various databases. We've selected a Recipes database here.

Filofax style
The app comes with three different visual 'skins' for your databases. As well as the leather-bound book look, you can also pick a clipboard or businesslike black look.

Field trip
All Bento's fields are customisable, and you can put whatever you like in each field. The on-screen keyboard appears when you want to edit text.

STEP BY STEP GUIDE: **Create a database in Bento**

1 Create record To begin creating a new database on the iPad, touch the 'Libraries' button at the top-left of Bento's screen, then tap the '+' sign. The next screen will show you template options.

2 What you want Flick through the available templates to select the most appropriate to your needs – in this case it's 'Home Inventory', but there are several to choose between.

3 Create Library With 'Home Inventory' at the centre of your Cover Flow-style display, simply touch the 'Create Library' button to get started.

4 Bento guides You'll see the database is pre-populated with one example, 'Laptop Computer'. Touch the record to explore the available fields and view a typical Bento entry.

5 Personal info   To change an entry in any record's field just touch the relevant item – 'Description' in this case. The on-screen keyboard will pop up and you can enter your new text.

6 Creative input   You can do the same for every field in your entry, creating an entirely personalised database. Edit, delete and add details with the iPad's virtual keyboard.

Desktop syncing

Desktop Bento 4 users can launch Bento on the Mac, touch the 'Sync' icon on the iPhone, then 'Sync Now' to sync the library. This ensures that your databases are always up to date whether you're on your Mac or your iPad. Hit the cog icon (top-left) of any Bento screen to set up a sync. Your computer will need to be on the same WiFi network as each other.

7 We want information   Once you've entered the correct information, hit 'Back' to return to the previous screen to input appropriate information in other fields.

8 Adding fields   To add another field just tap 'Fields', then '+' to access the 'New Field' chooser, choose a field and tap 'Create'. Custom databases are just a few taps away on the iPad.

Control your computer from anywhere with LogMeIn

LogMeIn Ignition puts your entire computer in the palm of your hand

THE iPAD IS DESIGNED TO BE A BRIDGE BETWEEN
your smartphone and your computer, and its portability
makes it more convenient on the go than a laptop.
However, there are times when you wish you had your
computer with you – if you need access to a file you
don't have on you, for example.

LogMeIn's Ignition app solves this problem by giving you remote access
to your computer on your iPad via the internet. The company offers several
products that do this. We'll focus on LogMeIn Ignition for the iPad here,
but they're all set up the same way. To start, go to **secure.logmein.com** and
download the LogMeIn Free software onto the computer you want to control.

As the name implies, this software is free, and you can download it onto
one or more Macs and PCs that you want to control remotely. For this
walkthough, we installed the software on our MacBook and then followed
the prompts to set up a free LogMeIn account on the company's website.

Once you've registered your Mac on the company's web page, it'll show you
the details of your LogMeIn account and the computers that you've set up for
remote access over the internet. You can use this web page to manage your
account, adjust settings and add other computers that you also want to control.

Then it's a question of downloading and installing LogMeIn Ignition on your
iPad in the same way as any other app. Once you've downloaded it, you're ready
to go with this tutorial.

KIT LIST:
- iPad
- Internet connection
- Mac or PC with LogMeIn Free installed (must be powered on and awake)
- LogMeIn Ignition iPad app, £17.99 from iTunes App Store

Time required: 20 mins
Difficulty: Intermediate

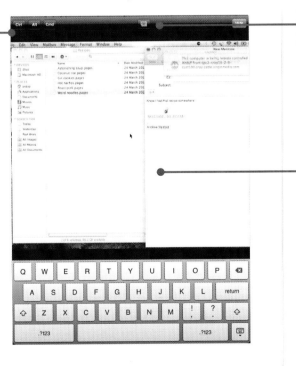

Mini me
This message appears on your computer's desktop and on your iPad so you know that the connection has been made. And if you're using your iPad to show someone how to do something on a remote computer, they'll know their computer isn't haunted.

Remote controls
Your main LogMeIn Ignition functions are covered here, from summoning the keyboard to logging in. As usual, the cog icon brings up settings, while the 'x' disconnects from the computer you're remote controlling.

Key skills
In keyboard mode, these buttons give you access to shortcut keys, so you can use your computer in much the same was as you would if it were sat in front of you.

Function keys
This button brings up the function keys when you're in virtual keyboard mode.

Access granted
LogMeIn has uses beyond tech support and showing mum how to use Spotify – the finder works just as it does on the desktop computer, so you can search for files and send them to yourself or someone else.

STEP BY STEP GUIDE: Remote control your computer

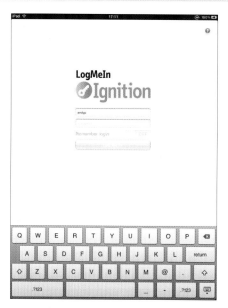

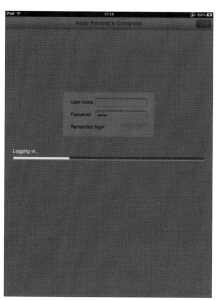

1 Logging in First make sure you've installed LogMeIn on your computer and set up an account. Instructions for this are on page 138. Then launch Ignition on your iPad and enter your details.

2 Helping hand Ignition displays the PCs and Macs you've added to your LogMeIn account (the computer has to be turned on). Tap the computer name and enter the computer's login details.

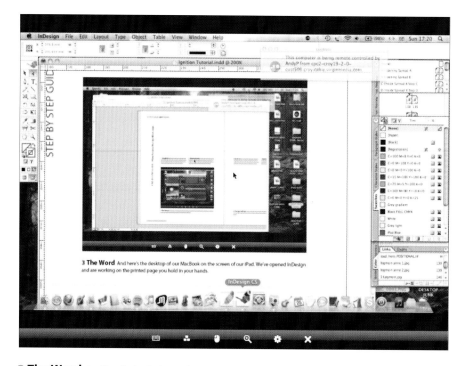

3 The Word And here's the desktop of our MacBook on the screen of our iPad. We've opened InDesign and are working on the printed page you hold in your hands.

4 Zoom in Now we're editing a document in Pages (the desktop version). Activate the on-screen keyboard to start typing. You can also zoom in and out by pinching with your fingers on the screen.

5 Keyboard commands Press the icon at the top of the screen in the middle to bring up your function keys, so on a Mac you can press F12 for Exposé. This also gives you arrow keys .

Mouse modes
There are two ways of using the cursor in LogMeIn Ignition. 'Mouse moves' mode treats the iPad screen like the trackpad on a laptop. In 'Screen moves' mode, the mouse cursor remains permanently fixed in the centre of the screen and the screen moves behind it. To select which one you want to use, tap the cog icon, then tap 'Scroll Mode'.

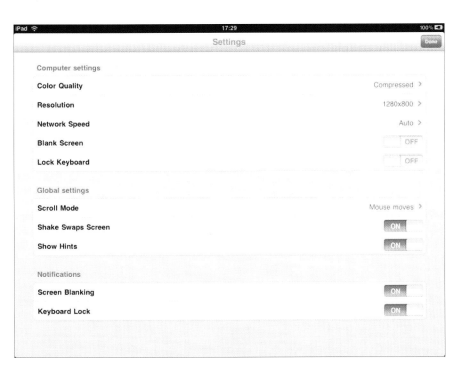

6 Change settings Click the cog icon in the Ignition dock to go to the settings screen. This window includes further options such as the ability to change the resolution of your Mac's screen.

Save web content for offline reading with Instapaper

Instapaper offers a simple way to bookmark internet content

HOW DO YOU ACCESS ONLINE CONTENT ON YOUR
iPad when you can't get online? WiFi hotspots aren't
as ubiquitous as we'd like, and even if you have the 3G
version of the iPad, there are still quite a few places, from
London Underground stations to rural dales, where you
won't be able to get a signal.

One solution would be to make good use of your online time by finding a
bunch of articles you want to read, then saving them in Safari as web archives
for offline reading. Wait a minute – Safari for the iPad doesn't have that feature.
Enter Instapaper, which essentially offers that missing functionality.

The app puts a button in Safari's bookmarks bar that you click whenever you
want to save a page for later. This creates a downloadable text-only version of
the article under your account name on the developer's website. Later, when
offline, you fire up the Instapaper app to read it.

Even if you're seldom offline, Instapaper can be a useful tool. Have you
ever bookmarked a series of articles to revisit when you have more time, then
struggled to find them weeks later in your overgrown thicket of a bookmarks list?
Instapaper makes this a no-brainer since, once you've registered with the site,
you're likely to keep using it to track pages you want to read later on.

There is a free Lite version of the app, but only the Pro version is listed as iPad-
compatible by the developer. It allows up to 250 pages to be saved and has folder
support, a dark mode for night reading and the ability to recommend articles.

KIT LIST:

- iPad
- Internet connection
  for web browsing
- Instapaper Pro app,
  £2.99 from iTunes
  App Store

Time required: 10 mins
Difficulty: Beginner

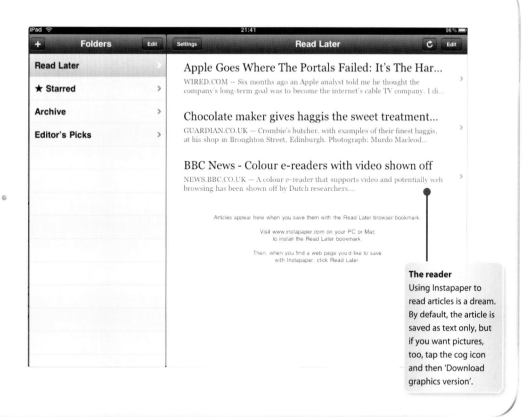

The reader
Using Instapaper to read articles is a dream. By default, the article is saved as text only, but if you want pictures, too, tap the cog icon and then 'Download graphics version'.

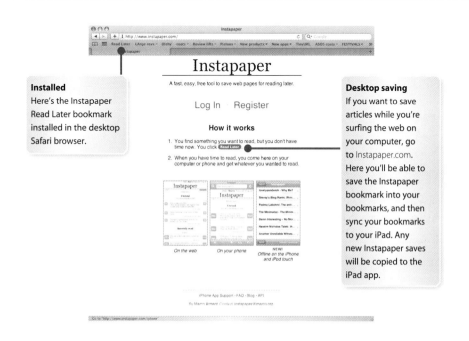

Installed
Here's the Instapaper Read Later bookmark installed in the desktop Safari browser.

Desktop saving
If you want to save articles while you're surfing the web on your computer, go to Instapaper.com. Here you'll be able to save the Instapaper bookmark into your bookmarks, and then sync your bookmarks to your iPad. Any new Instapaper saves will be copied to the iPad app.

STEP BY STEP GUIDE: Set up and use Instapaper

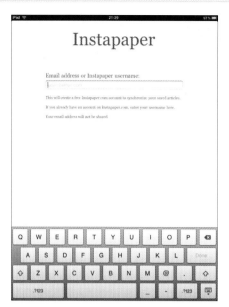

1 Open up Fire up Instapaper on your iPad and hit the 'Log in to Instapaper' button. You'll then be prompted to log in, or sign up if you've never used it before.

2 Sign in Registration is easy, and can be done on the Safari browser on your iPad, iPhone, iPod touch or computer. You just have to think of a username and enter it.

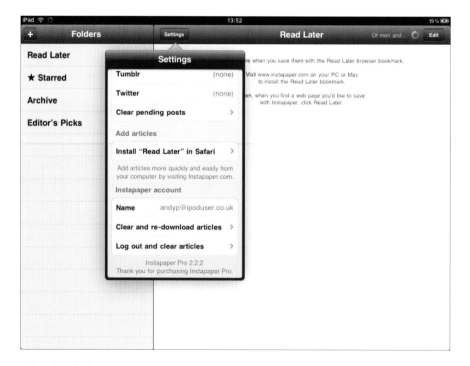

3 On the desktop You need to install the 'Read Later' bookmark in your iPad's browser. Go to Instapaper's settings and select 'Install Read Later in Safari'.

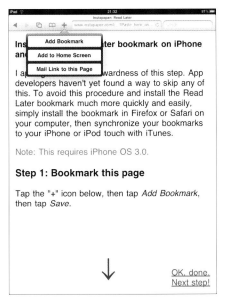

Ins... ... **...ter bookmark on iPhone and...**

I ap... ...wardness of this step. App developers haven't yet found a way to skip any of this. To avoid this procedure and install the Read Later bookmark much more quickly and easily, simply install the bookmark in Firefox or Safari on your computer, then synchronize your bookmarks to your iPhone or iPod touch with iTunes.

Note: This requires iPhone OS 3.0.

Step 1: Bookmark this page

Tap the "+" icon below, then tap *Add Bookmark*, then tap *Save*.

↓

OK, done.
Next step!

Select all of the text in this box and *Copy* it:

```
javascript:function
iprl5(){var
d=document,z=d.createEle
ment('scr'+'ipt'),b=d.body;tr
y{if(!b)throw(0);d.title='(Sav
ing...)
'+d.title;z.setAttribute('src',
'http://www.instapaper.com/
j/eEjT0kfpARdF?
u='+encodeURIComponent
(d.location.href)+'&t='+(ne
w
Date().getTime())));b.appen
```

1. Tap inside. The keyboard will appear.
2. Tap and hold for the magnifying glass, then release. *Select/Select All/Paste* will appear.
3. Tap *Select All*. *Cut/Copy/Paste* will appear.
4. Tap *Copy*.
5. Tap the *Done* button.

4 Create a bookmark This will launch Safari, and you'll be walked through how to create the special bookmark. You first create a bookmark for the page you're on.

5 Secret code Next, follow the instructions guide to edit your new bookmark's setup by going into the bookmark's URL and copying and pasting some code into it.

Desktop save

Setting up the Read Later bookmark on your desktop version of Safari is just a question of going to www. instapaper.com and dragging and dropping a ready-made bookmark to your Bookmark bar. Provided you then open Instapaper on the iPad when you're online (just before you leave the office, for example) and refresh it, your desktop internet finds will be available for you to read offline on the way home.

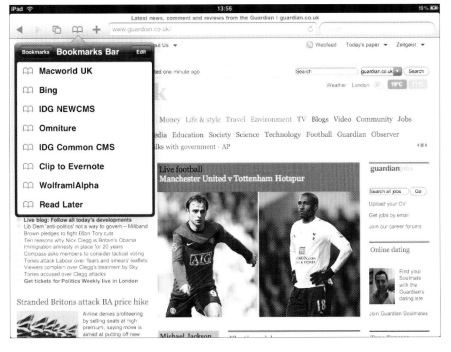

6 Save for later Now, when you browse in Safari, you can save an article for later by going to your bookmarks and selecting the 'Read Later' bookmark.

Create works of art with just your finger and your iPad

The iPad has many creative uses – Brushes lets you finger paint

BRUSHES IS A GREAT APPLICATION IF YOU WANT
to use your iPad to paint. It's so good that Jorge Colombo drew a cover for *The New Yorker* magazine with it on his iPhone while queuing outside Madame Tussauds.
Of course, the graphic designers among you might not be able to get by purely with work created on mobile devices, but you get the point – this is one clever app, and the iPad version is great.

Brushes takes advantage of the simple skill everyone has with finger painting, gives you a blank canvas, and lets you get going. It's intuitive yet surprisingly powerful, with three brush types, support for layers and the ability to handle a multiple undos, which means you can go back almost any number of steps if you go in the wrong creative direction.

You can base your painting on any image in your photo albums and export the result back to Photos. Even more impressive is the fact that Brushes can share your masterpieces – it has its own simple web server built in, which puts up a gallery of your work that can be viewed from any computer on the local network. And if you're on a Mac, you can also take delight in revisiting the mixture of toil, inspiration and plain messing around that gave life to your paintings: just export your work in Brushes' own .brushes format, then play back the result, step by crucial step, using the free Brushes Viewer application for Mac OS X.

Here we show you the basics of Brushes – including how to import a photo – and explore its colour and layer tools.

KIT LIST:

- iPad
- Some pictures synced to your iPad
- Brushes app, £2.99 from iTunes App Store

Time required: 20 mins
Difficulty: Beginner

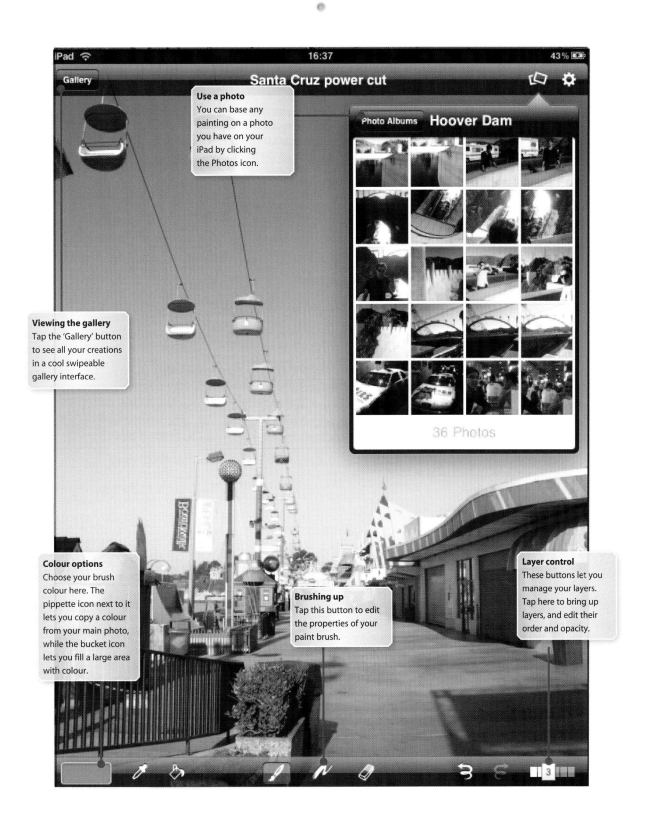

Gallery

Santa Cruz power cut

Use a photo
You can base any painting on a photo you have on your iPad by clicking the Photos icon.

Photo Albums **Hoover Dam**

36 Photos

Viewing the gallery
Tap the 'Gallery' button to see all your creations in a cool swipeable gallery interface.

Colour options
Choose your brush colour here. The pippette icon next to it lets you copy a colour from your main photo, while the bucket icon lets you fill a large area with colour.

Brushing up
Tap this button to edit the properties of your paint brush.

Layer control
These buttons let you manage your layers. Tap here to bring up layers, and edit their order and opacity.

STEP BY STEP GUIDE: **Learn to paint with Brushes**

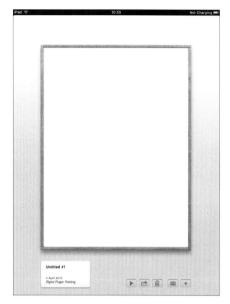

1 Starting your masterpiece You can start from a blank canvas. If you want it coloured, tap the colour selector in the bottom-right, pick a colour, then tap the paint bucket tool.

2 Import a picture Alternatively, you can start with a picture and edit it. Tap the pictures icon in the top right, and select a shot from the photo albums that are stored on your iPad.

3 Paint job Now you're ready. Choose your brush colour by tapping the colour box in the bottom-left. To copy a colour from your image, select the eye-dropper tool and drag the ring to the colour you want.

4 Select a brush The Brushes tool lets you vary the size of the brush with a slider. You can change the brush type using the three dots. You can zoom in and out of your image by pinching.

5 Layer it on We've painted this scary lake monster, and now want to add another picture. Tap the layers button (bottom-right), then tap '+'. Layers are useful for building up an image.

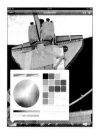

Using opacity
In the colour picker, it's possible to pick a colour and give it opacity. This means that your brush strokes will be see-through, to a degree that you set using the opacity slider – the bottom slider on the left of the colour picker.

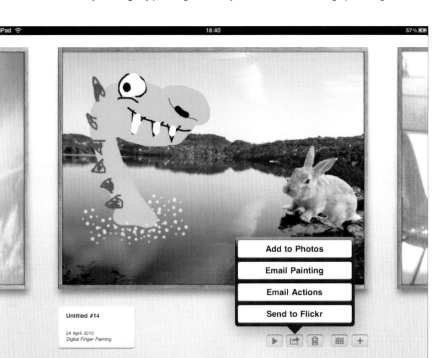

8 It's an art rage We imported another photo onto another layer, and feel that our work is done. Tap 'Gallery' (top-left), then the arrow button to see the options you have for saving and sending your art.

Make Twitter manageable with this great aggregator

Harness the power of Twitter with TweetDeck on your iPad

TWITTER ADDICTS SWEAR BY TWEETDECK ON THEIR
computers, and now this Twitter aggregator has an iPad
counterpart. The application allows you to handle all your
incoming and outgoing Tweets in one place, by giving you
an interface that brings each account together. The idea
is that you set up various 'columns' to display your Twitter
activity – for example, you'll have a column for your friends' tweets, tweets that
mention you by name, and your direct messages. You can add any number of
columns, based on user groups, Twitter searches and Twitter trends.

TweetDeck makes Twitter a lot easier to use, and the app makes your own
tweeting much easier, too, thanks to easy access to hashtags, contacts, pictures,
and more besides. The app works entirely independently on the iPad, but if
you use TweetDeck on the desktop, as well, it might be worth registering with
TweetDeck and getting an account (on top of your Twitter accounts). Doing
that will let you sync across all your TweetDeck apps – essentially meaning that
columns you set up on the desktop can be replicated on your iPad, and your
iPhone, too, if you're rocking the whole Apple gadget line-up.

The iPad version of TweetDeck is really easy to use – and is probably more
intuitive that its desktop cousin. However, it's icon-driven, so you may need to
experiment with your tapping before you find some features. That is of course
unless you read this tutorial, which should help you get started in no time. It's a
deep app that rewards plenty of playing, though.

KIT LIST:

- iPad
- Internet connection
- TweetDeck app,
  free from iTunes
  App Store
- TweetDeck on your
  desktop required
  for syncing; free
  www.tweetdeck.com

Time required: 10 mins
Difficulty: Beginner

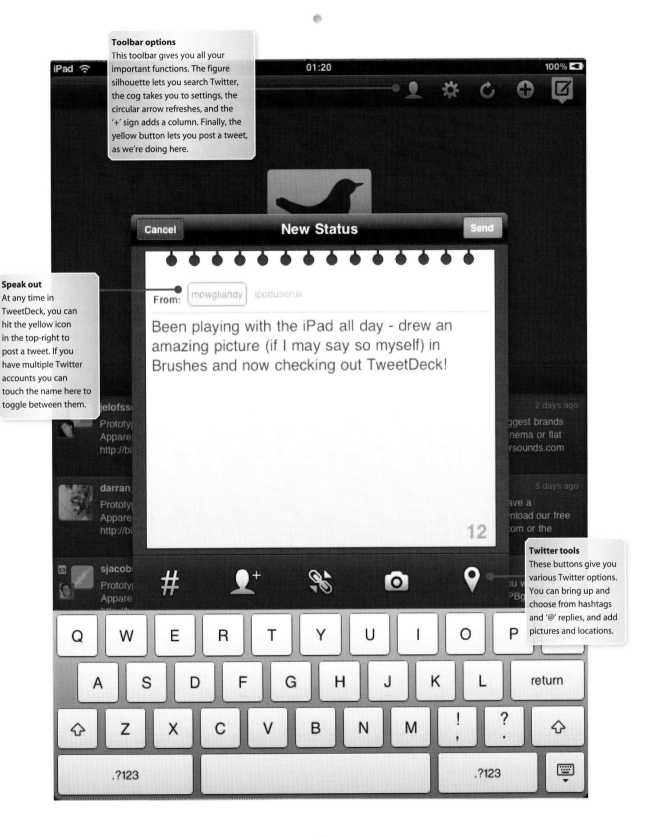

Toolbar options
This toolbar gives you all your important functions. The figure silhouette lets you search Twitter, the cog takes you to settings, the circular arrow refreshes, and the '+' sign adds a column. Finally, the yellow button lets you post a tweet, as we're doing here.

Speak out
At any time in TweetDeck, you can hit the yellow icon in the top-right to post a tweet. If you have multiple Twitter accounts you can touch the name here to toggle between them.

Cancel | **New Status** | Send

From: mowgliandy ipaduseruk

Been playing with the iPad all day - drew an amazing picture (if I may say so myself) in Brushes and now checking out TweetDeck!

12

Twitter tools
These buttons give you various Twitter options. You can bring up and choose from hashtags and '@' replies, and add pictures and locations.

STEP BY STEP GUIDE: How to use the TweetDeck

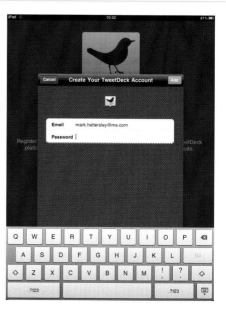

1 Blank canvas When you first launch
TweetDeck you'll see a blank 'No Columns'
message. Hit 'Twitter' in the middle of the
screen to add an account.

2 Get logged in Enter your details and tap
'Add' in the top-right. Once you're set up, you
can add more accounts later, if you like, so that
TweetDeck becomes your main app for Twitter.

3 Play columns Close the 'Settings' screen. Then hit the '+' at the top-right. Use the arrows to select
accounts and column types, then hit 'Add Column'.

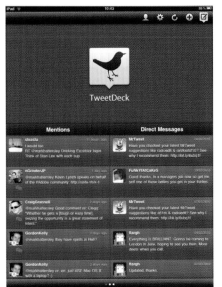

4 Tweet central You'll see the list of tweets as per your selections. Add more columns using the '+' button. To re-order your columns, tap and hold a column title.

5 Flick it Now you've got a few columns set up, you can flick between them. Tap one to zoom in on it. Tap the 'Columns' icon to choose another. To post a tweet, tap the yellow button (top-right).

Posting links

Twitter is a great way to share links with your friends, but URLs can take up too many of your 140 tweet characters. Bit.ly is a URL shortening site, and if you have an account, you can get TweetDeck to shorten URLs automatically. Sign up at http://bit.ly, then sign into your account in TweetDeck by tapping the cog icon and hitting 'Connect to Bit.ly'.

6 View updates The circular arrow icon in the top-right of the screen updates your columns. Tap a column heading to set how often the column updates of its own accord.

Keep on top of the tasks in your life with Things

This simple to-do list manager for the iPad is deceptively powerful

OVERWHELMED AND OVERWORKED? BELIEVE IT or not, your iPad can help relieve the pressure – and we don't mean by pumping Metallica into your ears at top volume at moments of high stress.

There is a multitude of task management apps on the App Store, but none are as simple and effective as Things. The idea is that you jot down tasks as and when you think of them, or when they come up, and then sort them out in a way that helps you meet your office targets, as well as remember your wedding anniversary. You can sort tasks into categories, create Projects, and even sync the app with a desktop version so you can keep on top of your tasks.

Things on the desktop (Mac only) is a slick and powerful task manager. It's expensive at a shade under £45, but if you're serious about getting on top of your workload, it's well worth a look. Things on the desktop gives you a system-wide keyboard shortcut for entering tasks into your inbox, so it won't interrupt what you're doing. To-dos can also have files, links, and contacts associated with them, just by dragging and dropping.

The iPad version is the perfect companion to the main desktop app, but it'll also serve you well if you use it by itself. It offers all the task-creation and management options of the desktop app in an intuitive interface. So, whether you're keeping track of your desktop to-do lists on the go or using your iPad as your main task manager, Things is bound to help you get on top of your life.

KIT LIST:
- iPad
- Things app, £11.99 from iTunes App Store
- Things app on your Mac optional; £44.95

Time required: 20 mins
Difficulty: Beginner

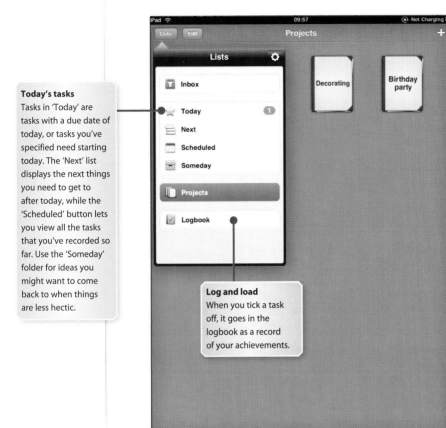

Plus points
A '+' button is on pretty much every Things screen, so you can quickly jot down a to-do before you forget it.

Today's tasks
Tasks in 'Today' are tasks with a due date of today, or tasks you've specified need starting today. The 'Next' list displays the next things you need to get to after today, while the 'Scheduled' button lets you view all the tasks that you've recorded so far. Use the 'Someday' folder for ideas you might want to come back to when things are less hectic.

Log and load
When you tick a task off, it goes in the logbook as a record of your achievements.

Desktop download
Things also syncs with a £45 desktop app. This gives you a bit more functionality, such as delegating tasks to contacts, and adding 'teammates' for tasks.

STEP BY STEP GUIDE: How to use Things

1 Open up When you fire up the app you'll see this empty home screen. This is where you can manage all your to-dos. Hit the '+' to add your first to-do.

2 Stuff to do Fill in the details of your task by tapping the corresponding fields to add due dates and notes. By default, all to-dos go in your 'Inbox' for sorting out later.

3 Tag it and bag it Hit 'Tags' to assign the task to a category – you can also add categories on this page if you want to. To create a custom tag, scroll to the bottom of the list and hit 'New tag'.

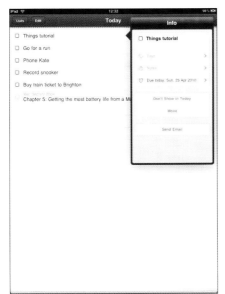

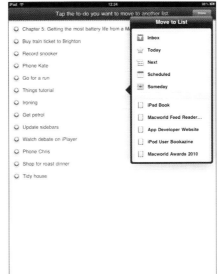

4 The day today Sort your tasks into the folders in the 'Lists' heading. All tasks with a due date of 'Today' automatically go into the 'Today' folder, to give you an overview of urgent tasks.

5 Priority calling The arrow icon at the top of a list's screen lets you move tasks between various folders. This is useful for prioritising items in your inbox and sorting them into a logical list.

Desktop tasks
You can use Things on the desktop to quickly log tasks while you work. To ensure your desktop Things gives you the same information as your iPad version, you can sync it over WiFi. To do this, you need to set it up on the desktop version. Go to Things → Preferences → Devices and follow the instructions. Your iPad will need to be on the same WiFi network as your computer.

6 Planning projects You can also create 'Projects', which lets you sort your tasks into areas. You can then move tasks from the inbox to a Project – great for breaking a big task into smaller chunks.

Interact with comics in a whole new way on your iPad

Comics as you've never seen them before – this app is a revelation

IF YOU'VE ALREADY DISCOVERED THE JOYS OF reading comics on your iPhone or iPod touch, you'll be blown away by the iPad version of the experience. There might be some doubt over which device is king of the mobile ebook readers, but there are no such uncertainties when it comes to comics: with its generously sized colour screen, the iPad was just made for the comics universe.

Of course there are plenty of apps to help you find your way around that realm, and among the coolest is the appropriately named Comics. It's a nifty comics reader, one that doesn't treat a comic as page after page of snazzy but inert art – not unless you insist on viewing comics that way.

Far more interesting is to double-tap on a page, taking you into Comics's 'Guided View' mode. Now the app shows you one panel at a time, letting each one occupy the whole screen while also zooming in to focus on speech balloons. It's terrific to see the app zigzag intelligently around each page to bring up the panels in the correct narrative sequence, though of course when it's doing its job really well, you'll be too engrossed in the story to notice.

Best of all, Comics even has its own iTunes-like store, allowing you to browse and buy from a vast library of online material, with stacks of worthwhile freebies available from cover to cover, too. Traditionalists need not feel put out: the app can suggest local specialist shops that may stock print versions of the very items you've seen in the virtual store.

KIT LIST:

- iPad
- Internet connection for buying comics
- Comics app, free from iTunes App Store

Time required: 10 mins
Difficulty: Beginner

Done
When you've finished reading a comic click the 'Close' button to return to the main menu.

To the left
Clicking on the left side of the screen moves back to the previous panel.

Central point
Clicking the central pane opens the options overlay.

To the right
Clicking on the right-hand side of the screen animates to the next panel.

STEP BY STEP GUIDE: Using the Comics app

1 Log in The first thing you need to do is create an account with ComiXology.com and log in. This will enable you to download new comics – some of which are free.

2 Search for a comic Now you can browse comics. You can search by 'Featured', 'Free', 'Top 25' or 'Browse' (which leads to options to search by Title, Creator, Publisher, and so on).

3 Pick a comic We're going to go for this *Clash Of The Titans* prequel. We found it in the 'Free' section. Click the button that says 'Free' to download it.

5 Read away Once downloaded the 'Free' button turns to 'Read'. Press it and the comic starts. Click the right-hand side to move through the panels.

6 Double tap The iPad is perfect for looking at the lush artwork of a decent comic – double-tap a frame to have it take up the whole screen. You can then navigate one frame at a time.

Adjust settings
Comics sports so many settings – from letterboxing and animated transitions – that it'll make you feel more like you're watching a partially animated movie than reading a comic. These are pretty cool but you can switch them off for a more regular experience. Click Settings ▸ Set Reading Preferences to see what can be changed.

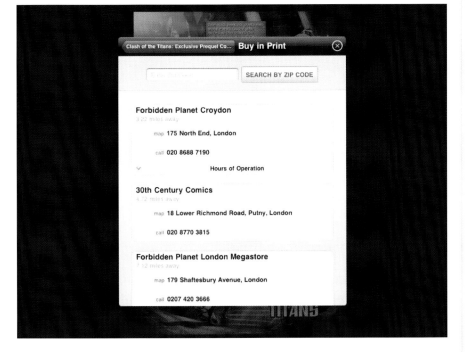

7 When you're done When you flick right from the last frame or page, you'll see a series of options – including the facility to look up local comic shops where you might be able to buy the one you just read.

The iPad challenge

With the first credible alternatives to the iPad starting to appear, Apple should be taking notes
By Andy Ihnatko

A couple of weeks ago, the first credible alternative to the iPad finally arrived in my office. The Motorola Xoom, like the iPad, is a 10in tablet running a mobile OS (Android 3.0). It's a nice piece of gear. It's no threat to the iPad but using it helped me to understand what makes the iPad work.

A tablet has to seem like one device, not like a computer that runs dozens of different apps. Using the Xoom, the one thing I missed about my iPad above all others was the sense that the hardware, the OS, and each of the two dozen or so apps I rely on were designed to work together.

Google doesn't understand that it has a responsibility to behave like an evil megacorporation that wants to crush all opposition. Google has many of the best and most popular web apps. So when I pick up a tablet that runs a Google OS and launch a Google-created web browser and navigate to a Google web app, I'm expecting a spectacular experience.

Instead, Google Reader identifies the Xoom as a mobile device and serves up the stripped-down edition. You don't even get the standard full web edition. Seriously.

Apple may be a tyrant, but when the company exerts control, it also imposes order and improves the overall experience. Google can't even be bothered to make its own web apps work well with its own OS. With an attitude like that, they'll never grind the huddled masses under their iron-studded boot heel.

If I see any threat to the iPad's supremacy, it's the £399 entry-level price. What'll happen if the market is flooded with perfectly decent £150 Android 3.0 tablets, and a lot of new money and users enter the Android Marketplace? I wonder.

It's important to remember that the iPad's dominance of the tablet market isn't the result of Divine Ordinance. There are reasons why the iPad works as well as it does and there are reasons why other devices could one day do just as well. If Apple overlooks either one of those things, it'll quickly become apparent that Apple never had a lock on the tablet market... just a two-year headstart.

> It's important to remember that the iPad's dominance of the tablet market isn't the result of Divine Ordinance